Disabilities

Series Editor: Cara Acred

Volume 255

Independence Educational Publishers

First published by Independence Educational Publishers

The Studio, High Green

Great Shelford

Cambridge CB22 5EG

England

© Independence 2014

Copyright

Photocopy licence

British Library Cataloguing in Publication Data

Disabilities. -- (Issues ; 255)

1. Disabilities--Great Britain. 2. People with
disabilities--Legal status, laws, etc.--Great Britain.
3. People with disabilities--Services for--Great Britain.
I. Series II. Acred, Cara editor of compilation.

362.4'0941-dc23

ISBN-13: 9781861686664

Printed in Great Britain
MWL Print Group Ltd

Contents

Introduction

Disabilities is Volume 255 in the *ISSUES* series. The aim of the series is to offer current, diverse information about important issues in our world, from a UK perspective.

ABOUT DISABILITIES

How do we define a 'disability'? What are some of the challenges facing disabled people in today's society? Are learning difficulties classed as disabilities? The new Disabilities book from the *ISSUES* series explores these questions, and more. It also looks at the rights of disabled people in the UK, financial issues and social prejudices.

OUR SOURCES

Titles in the *ISSUES* series are designed to function as educational resource books, providing a balanced overview of a specific subject.

The information in our books is comprised of facts, articles and opinions from many different sources, including:

⇨ Newspaper reports and opinion pieces

⇨ Website factsheets

⇨ Magazine and journal articles

⇨ Statistics and surveys

⇨ Government reports

⇨ Literature from special interest groups.

A NOTE ON CRITICAL EVALUATION

Because the information reprinted here is from a number of different sources, readers should bear in mind the origin of the text and whether the source is likely to have a particular bias when presenting information (or when conducting their research). It is hoped that, as you read about the many aspects of the issues explored in this book, you will critically evaluate the information presented.

It is important that you decide whether you are being presented with facts or opinions. Does the writer give a biased or unbiased report? If an opinion is being expressed, do you agree with the writer? Is there potential bias to the 'facts' or statistics behind an article?

ASSIGNMENTS

In the back of this book, you will find a selection of assignments designed to help you engage with the articles you have been reading and to explore your own opinions. Some tasks will take longer than others and there is a mixture of design, writing and research-based activities that you can complete alone or in a group.

FURTHER RESEARCH

At the end of each article we have listed its source and a website that you can visit if you would like to conduct your own research. Please remember to critically evaluate any sources that you consult and consider whether the information you are viewing is accurate and unbiased.

Useful weblinks

www.assistancedogs.org.uk

www.autism.org.uk

www.cerebra.org.uk

www.cost-ofliving.net

www.disabilityrightsuk.org

www.dyslexiaaction.org.uk

www.mencap.org.uk

www.ncb.org.uk

www.nhs.uk

www.scope.org.uk

Life with a disability

Disabled people are often talked about as though they form one group, but every disabled person faces different challenges and health conditions.

The Equality Act 2010 defines a disabled person as anyone who has a physical or mental impairment that has a substantial and long-term adverse effect on his or her ability to carry out day-to-day activities. These impairments include:

⇨ loss of limbs

⇨ multiple sclerosis

⇨ heart disease

⇨ Down's syndrome

⇨ learning difficulties

⇨ mental health problems, such as depression and anxiety.

Older people are more likely to develop a disability and most disabled people are adults. More than ten million people in the UK are disabled, 770,000 of whom are children.

More people are living with a disability now than in the past because we're living longer, and improved medical treatments are enabling more people to manage long-term health problems. The Equality and Human Rights Commission says that 58% of people over 50 will have a long-term health condition by 2020.

Independence with the right support

Disabilities of any kind present challenges, but this doesn't mean that life with a disability can't be fulfilling.

For most people, a fulfilling life means having control over their day-to-day activities and being able to choose how they live.

More than one million disabled people live alone in the UK, and many more lead independent lives with help. For a lot of people, independent life also means being employed. Half of the UK's disabled people are in jobs, but it should be more. Only 17% of disabled people are born with their disability. Most disabled people have had to adjust to their disability as adults.

Caring for carers

It's not just disabled people who are challenged by disability, but also the people who care for them. The term 'carer' describes people who care for others on an unpaid basis, as opposed to people who are paid, such as care workers and home helps.

There are six million carers in the UK. If you're one of them, you may be entitled to support, such as help with caring, home adaptations and equipment, and short breaks from caring.

There's lots of practical advice as well as financial, legal and rights information for carers available from the Carers Direct website or on freephone 0808 802 0202.

20 January 2012

⇨ The above information is reprinted with kind permission from NHS Choices. Please visit www.nhs.uk for further information.

I think you'd better care for my carer today!

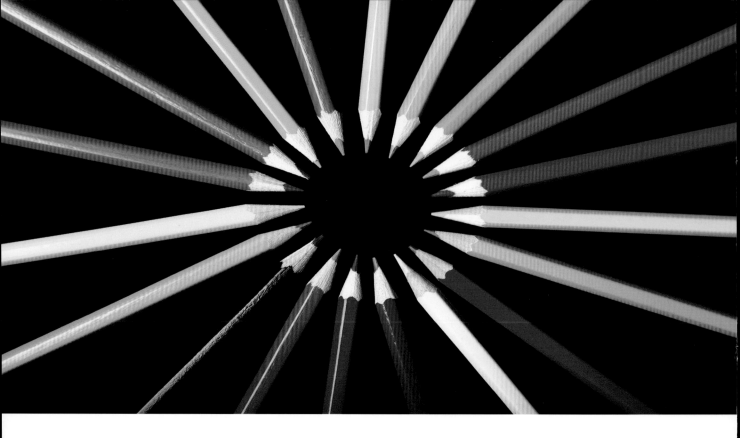

What is a learning disability?

A learning disability is a reduced intellectual ability and difficulty with everyday activities – for example household tasks, socialising or managing money – which affects someone for their whole life.

People with a learning disability tend to take longer to learn and may need support to develop new skills, understand complex information and interact with other people.

The level of support someone needs depends on individual factors, including the severity of their learning disability. For example, someone with a mild learning disability may only need support with things like getting a job. However, someone with a severe or profound learning disability may need full-time care and support with every aspect of their life – they may also have physical disabilities.

People with certain specific conditions can have a learning disability too. For example, people with Down's syndrome and some people with autism have a learning disability.

Learning disability is often confused with dyslexia and mental health problems. Mencap describes dyslexia as a 'learning difficulty' because, unlike learning disability, it does not affect intellect. Mental health problems can affect anyone at any time and may be overcome with treatment, which is not true of learning disability.

It's important to remember that with the right support, most people with a learning disability in the UK can lead independent lives.

Causes

A learning disability occurs when the brain is still developing – before, during or soon after birth.

⇨ Before birth, things can happen to the central nervous system (the brain and spinal cord) that can cause a learning disability. A child can be born with a learning disability if the mother has an accident or illness while she is pregnant, or if the unborn baby develops certain genes. Genes are chemicals in our bodies that contain information about us – like how we look.

⇨ A person can be born with a learning disability if he or she does not get enough oxygen during childbirth, or is born too early.

⇨ After birth, a learning disability can be caused by early childhood illnesses.

Getting a diagnosis of learning disability

A learning disability can be diagnosed at any time. A child may be diagnosed at birth, or a parent or professional may notice a difference in their development during early childhood. For some people it may be many years before they receive a diagnosis – while others may never receive a diagnosis at all.

Even with a diagnosis, it is often not possible to say why someone has a learning disability.

'We've heard from a lot of parents how difficult the experience of diagnosis can be, especially when there are still so many uncertainties about the future. But there is a lot of support and information available, and lots of reasons to be optimistic about the future.'

Although getting a diagnosis can be a very difficult and emotional experience for families, it is often the first step to accessing the care and support they need for the future.

Learning disability and other conditions

Some people with a learning disability also have other physical and emotional conditions, and may receive more than one diagnosis. This could have an impact on the kind of support they and their families need in their day-to-day life. You can find out more about some of the conditions associated with learning disability below.

Autism and Asperger syndrome

We hear from many parents who think their child may have autism, or who have just received a diagnosis and are looking for help and support.

Challenging behaviour

Some people with a learning disability may demonstrate extreme behaviour, which is often referred to as challenging behaviour.

Cerebral palsy

Someone with cerebral palsy may also have a learning disability.

Down's syndrome

Down's syndrome is a genetic condition. It is often diagnosed shortly after birth due to the physical characteristics associated with it.

Fragile X syndrome

Fragile X is a genetic condition that affects both boys and girls, although boys are often more severely affected.

Global development delay

The term 'developmental delay' or 'global development delay' is used when a child takes longer to reach certain developmental milestones than other children their age.

A parent's story: global development delay

During pregnancy my wife received all the normal antenatal check ups. We weren't really given any information, except for a mis-diagnosis that scared the hell out of us.

Other conditions

There are a number of other conditions that can result in someone having a learning disability.

Facts about learning disability

Most people with a learning disability are treated as 'different'. They do not have the same control over their own lives as the rest of our society and face challenges and prejudice every day.

⇨ Less than one in five people with a learning disability work (compared with one in two disabled people generally), but we know that at least 65% of people with a learning disability want to work. Of those people with a learning disability that do work, most only work part time and are low paid.

⇨ Just one in three people with a learning disability take part in some form of education or training.

⇨ Children with a learning disability are often socially excluded and eight out of ten children with a learning disability are bullied.

⇨ One in two families with a disabled child live in poverty.

⇨ At least half of all adults with a learning disability live in the family home – meaning that many don't get the same chances as other people to gain independence, learn key skills and make choices about their own lives.

⇨ 58,000 people with a learning disability are supported by day care services.

⇨ People with a learning disability are 58 times more likely to die aged under 50 than other people. And four times as many people with a learning disability die of preventable causes as people in the general population.

⇨ 75% of GPs have received no training to help them treat people with a learning disability.

⇨ Less than a third of people with a learning disability have some choice of who they live with, and less than half have some choice over where they live.

⇨ Seven out of ten families caring for someone with profound and multiple learning disabilities have reached or come close to 'breaking point' because of a lack of short-break services.

⇨ 29,000 adults with a learning disability live with parents aged 70 or over, many of whom are too old or frail to continue in their caring role. In only one in four of these cases have local authorities planned alternative housing.

Mencap is here to make sure people with a learning disability have the chance to change the world they live in and live their lives as they choose.

⇨ The above information is reprinted with kind permission from Mencap. Please visit www.mencap.org.uk for further information.

© Mencap 2013

Dyslexia and dyscalculia

About dyslexia

Dyslexia is a specific learning difficulty that affects approximately 10% of the UK population to varying degrees.

A working definition of dyslexia, as formulated by the Rose Review's Expert Advisory Group, is that dyslexia is a learning difficulty that primarily affects the skills involved in accurate and fluent word reading and spelling, which occurs across the range of intellectual abilities. Characteristic features of dyslexia are difficulties in phonological awareness, verbal memory and verbal processing speed. It is best thought of as a continuum, not a distinct category, and there are no clear cut-off points. Co-occurring difficulties may be seen in aspects of language, motor co-ordination, mental calculation, concentration and personal organisation, but these are not, by themselves, markers of dyslexia. A good indication of the severity and persistence of dyslexic difficulties can be gained by examining how the individual responds or has responded to well-founded intervention.

The impact of dyslexia is extensive: if you cannot learn to read, you cannot read to learn and everything we do at school and throughout life requires us to have the skills to be able to read fluently and accurately. Above and beyond the difficulties and barriers that dyslexia presents, is the damage that low self-esteem can cause.

However, with the right help and support, strategies to overcome difficulties associated with dyslexia can be learnt and dyslexia needn't be a barrier to achievement.

Dyslexia Action offers a wide range of help, support and advice. If you are concerned that you, a friend or a family member may be dyslexic you will need to get an assessment.

General indicators of dyslexia

Dyslexia can affect different people in different ways and its effects can range from mild to severe.

The list below provides an overview of the types of difficulties a dyslexic person may have at different ages and may be used as a guide to spotting indicators of dyslexia. It is not an exhaustive list, and it is not intended as a screening tool or diagnostic assessment. If you are worried that you, your partner, a friend or a family member may be dyslexic, you should contact your nearest Dyslexia Action centre to arrange an assessment.

Ages seven to 11:

⇨ Seems bright in some ways but unexpectedly struggles in others

⇨ Other members of the family have similar difficulties

⇨ Has difficulties carrying out three instructions in sequence

⇨ Struggles to learn sequences such as days of the week or the alphabet

⇨ Is a slow reader or makes unexpected errors when reading aloud

⇨ Often reads a word, then fails to recognise it further down the page

⇨ Struggles to remember what has been read

⇨ Puts letters and numbers the wrong way: for example, 15 for 51, b for d or 'was' for 'saw'

⇨ Has poor handwriting and/or struggles to hold the pen/pencil correctly and/or learn cursive writing

⇨ Spells a word several different ways

⇨ Appears to have poor concentration

⇨ Struggles with mental arithmetic or learning times tables

⇨ Seems to struggle with maths and/or understanding the terminology in maths: for example, knowing when to add, subtract or multiply

⇨ Has difficulties understanding time and tense

⇨ Confuses left and right

⇨ Can answer questions orally but has difficulties writing the answer down

⇨ Has trouble learning nursery rhymes or songs

⇨ Struggles with phonics and learning the letter to sound rules

⇨ Seems to get frustrated or suffers unduly with stress and/ or low self-esteem

⇨ Struggles to copy information down when reading from the board

⇨ Needs an unexpected amount of support with homework and struggles to get it done on time

⇨ Is excessively tired after a day at school.

Ages 12 to adult

Many older children and adults will remember having similar difficulties to those listed above and some may still apply into adulthood, but some additional issues for older children through to adults might include:

⇨ Difficulties taking notes

⇨ Difficulties planning and writing essays, letters or reports

⇨ Difficulties reading and understanding new terminology

⇨ Quality of work is erratic

⇨ Difficulties revising for examinations

⇨ Struggles to communicate knowledge and understanding in exams

⇨ Feels that the effort put in does not reflect performance or results

⇨ Forgets names and factual information, even when familiar

⇨ Struggles to remember things such as a personal PIN or telephone number

⇨ Struggles to meet deadlines

⇨ Struggles with personal organisation (finances/ household, arrives at lessons with the wrong books, forgets appointments)

⇨ Difficulties filling in forms or writing cheques

⇨ Only reads when necessary and never for pleasure

⇨ Develops work avoidance tactics to disguise difficulties

and/or worries about being promoted/taking professional qualifications

⇨ Difficulties become exacerbated when under pressure of time.

Dyscalculia

Dyscalculia is now a recognised type of specific learning difficulty, although less is known about it compared with dyslexia.

There is a now substantial amount of evidence that people experience a range of specific difficulties with the learning, retention and application of mathematical skills and related reasoning abilities. It would appear that dyslexia and dyscalculia can be co-occurring conditions, although each can exist without the other being present.

In order to assess for the presence of dyscalculia/maths difficulties it is important to investigate a range of underlying ability areas, such as working memory, language, visual reasoning, information processing, etc. in order to appraise a person's profile of strengths and weaknesses. Literacy and mathematical skills also need to be assessed jointly in order to make judgements about the extent and severity of a person's difficulties. It is always important not to prejudge the nature of a person's apparent learning difficulties and

so the assessment framework needs to be dynamic and enquiring in style.

There is a considerable body of research to indicate that children, young people and adults with dyscalculia/maths difficulties can respond positively to well-organised teaching inputs from suitably qualified and experienced teachers. These inputs often don't have to be extremely specialised and sometimes it is difficult to distinguish 'dyscalculia' from the sorts of common mathematical difficulties that everyone experiences from time to time in their learning. This is particularly true for young children within KS1 and KS2. What is important is that a person's particular weaknesses and strengths are identified and that an individual programme of support is carefully designed, implemented and monitored over time by a skilled teacher. Dyslexia Action can provide high-quality assessment and teaching in the area of dyscalculia/maths difficulties in all of its centres.

⇨ The above information is reprinted with kind permission from Dyslexia Action. Please visit www.dyslexiaaction.org. uk for further information.

© Dyslexia Action 2013

Autism and Asperger syndrome

Autism and Asperger syndrome are both part of a range of related developmental disorders known as autism spectrum disorders (ASD). They begin in childhood and last through adulthood.

ASD can cause a wide range of symptoms, which are grouped into three categories:

⇨ problems and difficulties with social interaction – including lack of understanding and awareness of other people's emotions and feelings

⇨ impaired language and communication skills – including delayed language development and an inability to start conversations or take part in them properly

⇨ unusual patterns of thought and physical behaviour – including making repetitive physical movements, such as hand tapping or twisting (the child develops set routines of behaviour and can get upset if the routines are broken).

There is currently no cure for ASD. However, a wide range of treatments, including specialist education and behavioural programmes, can help improve symptoms.

In England, it is estimated that one in every 100 children has an ASD. The conditions are more common in boys than girls. Boys are three to four times more likely to develop an ASD than girls.

Types of ASD

The term 'spectrum' is used because the symptoms of ASD can vary from person to person and range from mild to severe.

It is also common for children with ASD to have symptoms or aspects of other conditions such as:

⇨ attention deficit hyperactivity disorder (ADHD)

⇨ Tourette's syndrome or other tic disorders

⇨ epilepsy

⇨ dyspraxia (developmental co-ordination disorder).

There are three main types of ASD:

⇨ autistic disorder, sometimes known as 'classic autism'

⇨ Asperger syndrome

⇨ pervasive developmental disorder – not otherwise specified (PDD-NOS), also known as 'atypical autism'.

Autistic disorder

Children with autistic disorder usually have significant problems with language, social interaction and behaviour. Many children with autistic disorder also have learning difficulties and below-average intelligence.

Asperger syndrome

Children with Asperger syndrome have milder symptoms that affect social interaction and behaviour. Their language development is usually not affected. However, they often have problems in certain areas of language, such as understanding humour or figures of speech ('It's raining cats and dogs', for example).

Children with Asperger syndrome usually have intelligence within the normal range. Some children have particular skills in areas that require logic, memory and creativity, such as maths, computer science and music.

Pervasive developmental disorder – not otherwise specified

PDD-NOS is diagnosed in children who share some, but not all, of the traits of autistic disorder or Asperger syndrome.

Most children with PDD-NOS have milder symptoms than children with autistic disorder, but they do not share the language skills and normal range of intelligence associated with Asperger syndrome.

Autism in children

Autism can normally be diagnosed in children at around the age of two. However, it can be difficult to diagnose as the symptoms will often only become more noticeable as the children get older.

See your GP if you notice any of the symptoms of ASD or if you're concerned about your child's development. You can discuss your concerns together in depth before deciding whether your child should be referred for a specialist assessment.

If your child is diagnosed with ASD, there will be many things to consider as a parent, including coping with daily life at home and choosing the right school. Read a parent's guide to autism for more information about coping with your child's diagnosis.

Autism in adults

Some people with ASD grow up without ever being diagnosed, sometimes through choice. However, getting a diagnosis of ASD as an adult can often help people with ASD and their families understand the condition and work out what kind of support they need.

A range of autism-specific services is available to help adults with ASD find advice and support, get involved in leisure activities and find somewhere they are comfortable living.

Some adults with ASD may also have difficulty finding a job because of the social demands and changes in routine that working involves. However, they can get support to help them find a job that matches their abilities and skills.

Are rates of autism increasing?

The number of diagnosed cases of ASD has increased over the past 20 years, but this does not necessarily mean that the condition is becoming more widespread.

Some experts argue that the rise in diagnosed cases may be due to health professionals getting better at diagnosing cases correctly. In the past, many children with an ASD may have been incorrectly labelled as 'slow', 'difficult' or 'painfully shy', and not given the treatment they needed.

Some campaigners believe that the rise in cases is due to the MMR (mumps, measles and rubella) vaccine.

The MMR vaccine has been investigated extensively in a number of major studies around the world, involving millions of children. Researchers have found no evidence of a link between MMR and ASD.

In 2009, one of the country's leading ASD charities, the National Autism Society, released a statement supporting the claim that there is no link between MMR and ASD.

In the US, a compound containing mercury called thiomersal, which is used as a preservative in some vaccines, has also been claimed to cause ASD.

Thiomersal has been extensively studied and no evidence of a link to ASD has been found. Furthermore, thiomersal was removed from vaccines in the US after 1999, yet the rates of ASD have continued to rise.

Outlook

Children with moderate symptoms who have average or above-average intelligence often grow up to be independent adults with jobs, long-term relationships and children.

Children with more severe symptoms who have below-average intelligence are likely to find it difficult to live independently as adults and may need additional care and assistance. However, there is no reason why they cannot enjoy a good quality of life.

2 March 2012

⇨ The above information is reprinted with kind permission from NHS Choices. Please visit www.nhs.uk for further information.

© NHS Choices 2012

What are the issues facing people with autism?

People on the autism spectrum and their relatives and carers face many issues, and some problems, on a day-to-day basis.

This article identifies some of the most common issues and problems. However it is important to remember that each autistic person is a unique individual, with unique needs and abilities. Because of this, he or she will experience those issues in a unique way or may not experience them at all.

It is just as important to remember that some individuals with autism don't think of autism as an issue at all, it's just the way they are.

Autism is not a problem

'People need to get over the idea that the neuro-typical way is "right" and any other way is "wrong". The AS way is just as valid, in fact better in some respect. We should be accepted in our own right and the emphasis should be on educating NTs not to be so discriminatory and to get over the absurd and offensive idea that they are better then anyone else. People with AS don't need to be "cured" or trained as to how to "pretend" to be normal, it is the "normal" people who need to learn that, contrary to what they think, they are not the pinnacle of God's creation and that there is in fact a lot they could learn from Aspies. They need to be taught not to be prejudiced and discriminatory and to accept and accommodate us for who we are.'

(Quoted in Beardon, L and Edmonds, G. (2007). ASPECT Consultancy Report. A national report on the needs of adults with Asperger syndrome. Sheffield: Sheffield Hallam University.)

Triad of impairments

People on the autism spectrum are reported to have difficulties with three main activities, sometimes known as the triad of impairments.

⇨ Social difficulties and autism. For example, they may take longer to learn to speak, or find it hard to begin or carry on a conversation.

⇨ Communication difficulties and autism. For example, they may not understand facial expressions or body language, or not be able to share things or feelings with other people.

⇨ Imagination difficulties and autism. For example, they may be extremely good at learning facts and figures but find it hard to discuss religion or politics.

They also demonstrate a narrow, repetitive range of activities. For example, they may develop an overwhelming interest in something, follow inflexible routines or rituals, or make repetitive body movements.

Secondary issues

Many people with autism are reported to have secondary difficulties, i.e. issues not symptomatic of autism but very common in people with autism. For example, many people with autism appear to have:

⇨ challenging behavioural problems, such as aggression and self-injury

⇨ mental health problems, such as anxiety or depression

⇨ sleep disorders, such as insomnia

- ⇨ sensory issues, such as hyper or hypo sensitivity

- ⇨ gastro-intestinal problems, such as diarrhoea.

Other conditions and syndromes

Most people on the autistic spectrum are reported to have additional conditions and syndromes which bring their own problems and which complicate the issues caused by autism. For example:

- ⇨ A significant minority of people with autism spectrum disorders also develop epilepsy

- ⇨ About a third of individuals with autism have some other learning disability

- ⇨ A significant minority of people with autism have some form of attention deficit hyperactivity disorder.

Integrating into society

Most people on the autism spectrum find it hard to integrate into society. For example, they may struggle to:

- ⇨ find or keep a job

- ⇨ run a home by themselves

- ⇨ begin or maintain a relationship.

Relatives and carers

Relatives and carers of people with autism also face issues and problems. For example they may:

- ⇨ carry the the worry and exhaustion of looking after someone with autism

- ⇨ face the frustration of trying to cope with other people's ignorance and prejudice – a problem also faced by people with autism themselves

- ⇨ become frustrated by the lack of high-quality information about interventions that can help

- ⇨ become frustrated by the poor quality of the services designed to help them.

Practical solutions to the issues and problems

As Temple Grandin, a woman with autism says, there is no 'one-size fits all' solution to the issues faced by people with autism. What works for one person may not work for another.

'People are always looking for the single magic bullet that will totally change everything. There is no single magic bullet.'

This article aims to provide information about some of the interventions used to help overcome some of these issues.

You may also find it useful to look at the Useful resources section of our website. Here you will find organisations and other resources that may help you tackle some of the issues.

4 February 2013

- ⇨ The above information is reprinted with kind permission from Research Autism. Please visit www.researchautism.net for further information.

© Research Autism 2013

How much does it cost to raise a disabled child?

Extra costs shopping list

Costs for a disabled child	Costs for a non-disabled child
A month's worth of pull-up nappies and wipes for a five-year-old disabled child: £60	A month's worth of pull-up nappies for a non-disabled five-year-old child: £0
Specially made car safety seat: £600	High-back car booster seat, from: £149.99
Specially measured sandals for eight-year-old disabled child: £120	Sandals for a non-disabled child, from a high-street shoe shop: £34
Sensory wooden toy: £1,000	Wooden blocks in a wagon toy, from a toy superstore: £16.99
Specially adapted bicycle for 11-year-old boy: £800	Bicycle for non-disabled 11-year-old boy: £79
Seamless socks: £6 a pair	Pack of five white children's socks from a supermarket: £2 for a pack of five, or 40p a pair
Special 'pea pod' supportive bean bag: £385	Beanbag with cotton cover: £24.99
Touchscreen computer – essential for school work: £800	Computer: £259.99
Specialist mouse for computer: £200	Mouse for computer: £19.99
Big Keys keyboard for computer: £150	Keyboard: £39.99
TOTAL: £4,121	**TOTAL: £624.98**

Data collected from a range of families with disabled children

Source: Counting the Costs 2012, The financial reality for families with disabled children across the UK. *© Contact a Family, May 2012*

Time to tackle labels in society

Do you have a disability or a DISability?

It is almost funny to think of the old cliché of the 'glass half empty or half full' and to apply it to the way we view people with any kind of minor form of special needs in this country. Be it physical or psychological, we don't focus on what the person can do; which nine times out of ten is probably the same as everyone else, or maybe even above others in certain areas. Instead, we highlight the person's DISability to do something. Personally I think we need to start viewing people with special needs as having disABILITIES.

I write this piece looking from the inside out, since I am a 17-year-old with Asperger syndrome. This is a form of autism where people have normal, or often above normal intelligence, but can struggle with anxiety, social skills and other aspects of day-to-day life. If you met me, you would likely never know that I had it – I am sociable, funny (or so I like to think!) and just as intelligent as the next individual you would meet. I was fortunate, unlike many others, and benefited from early intervention. As a result, I am really enjoying my life to the max. However, I have seen first hand the effect that labels have.

So what are labels and who gives them out? Well, in some respects, we all need labels. For example, I needed diagnosis to get access to the services I needed for my condition; sick people need diagnosis for treatment; and young people need to be recognised in order to access appropriate education. However, when we start to get vague and generalise, the problems really set in. All too often, the media writes vaguely about 'young people' or 'the disabled' without really looking at individuals. Instead, they use broad brush strokes to tar everyone with the same brush – you can no more say that all Irish people are drunk fools and look like leprechauns, than you can say that all people with special needs are stupid or that all young people are trouble makers.

Laws are often passed to help people with special needs, but this is like a massive gazebo rather than an individual umbrella. While we can probably all remember spending time in school celebrating diversity, the system often seems to fail to explain that you can never generalise, but instead leaves issues such as special needs as vague as possible, probably due to time constraints and to avoid offending anybody.

Sadly, the effect of this breakdown in communication is easy to see. It can often be hilarious when someone finds out for the first time that you have special needs. On many occasions, I have been at parties and other events having a perfectly normal conversation with an individual when they find out that I have a condition. I then have to watch as they proceed to speak to me like I am deaf or only have very basic English! Yet, we cannot blame individuals for this crisis, because I know that every person who has tried to communicate to me as though they were speaking to E.T. does so with the best of intentions. They simply heard the word DISability and (due to their lack of knowledge of the topic) bunched my disABILITY in with the thousands of others across the globe into this one nice vague term the media and state can use for everything – a kind of one-size-fits-all approach that is too often used against us young people as a whole.

However, I know that labels are not only thrown at those with special needs. How often have you heard sweeping statements like 'those young people' or 'all travellers' or perhaps most horrifically recently when we saw an appalling generalisation thrown at the Polish community in Ireland by a judge.

All of this being said though, I think that we have a huge amount to be optimistic about. What always pleases me is how my own friends and classmates seem to embrace individuals on their own merits rather than on any label traditionally associated with them. I think we young Irish really are the generation who could break the age-old tradition that has evolved little since medieval ironsmiths' brand.

I also think that we should use forums such as President Higgins's 'Being Young and Irish' Seminar and bodies such as Comhairle na nÓg to really challenge the media, state, and, yes, even ourselves to look at individuals and not name tags. If we do that, then I think we really will help bring mega social change to Ireland. This will benefit every single person, as everyone gets tagged at some point!

7 October 2013

⇨ The above information is reprinted with kind permission from SpunOut.ie. Please visit www. spunout.ie for further information.

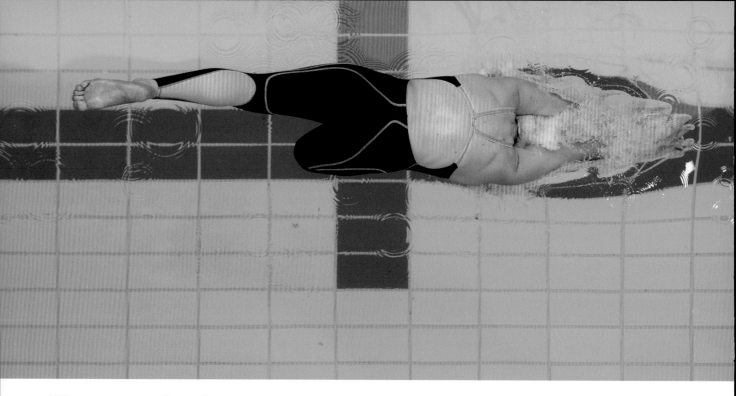

From victims to heroes to scroungers: changes in the public perception of disabled people

By Sasha Scambler

Disability and disabled people have regularly featured in the media over the past few months. Radio 4 is currently running a series exploring disability across history, we have had extensive coverage of the Oscar Pistorius court case in South Africa and disabled people feature in many of the scare stories about the NHS that are circulating. Underlying all of this are changes in the way that disability and disabled people are viewed within the media and by the general public.

In 2011, the World Health Organization published the first *World Report on Disability*. They estimated that more than one billion people across the world, approximately 15% of the population, live with a disability. A rise in numbers from the 1970s is accounted for by the ageing population and the increasing number of people living with long-term disabling conditions. Considering the UK, one in ten people live with a disability – the

most common being rheumatoid arthritis. The evidence from the WHO suggests that disabled people experience poorer health outcomes, lower educational achievement, increased levels of dependency and restricted participation in society, have lower employment rates and are more likely to live in poverty than their non-disabled peers. Disability activists say disabled people are consistently discriminated against, oppressed and stopped from achieving their potential in a world designed for non-impaired bodies.

Yet against this backdrop there is no universal understanding of the concept of 'disability'. The nature, meaning and impact of disability depend on the geographical, historical, social, cultural and economic environments in which the person with the disability is located. In addition to being culturally specific the concept of disability is also historically specific and the treatment of people with disabilities has changed over time.

Recognition and understanding of the changing nature of disability is essential to developing an understanding of disability today. This is particularly relevant when looking at changes in the popular view of disability and disabled people in the UK over the past few years. The image of disabled people as tragic victims in need of care and pity was replaced briefly (albeit in a very limited way) by a more positive focus on equality and the achievements of disabled athletes in the Paralympics. This was then replaced by the current focus on disability as a refuge of benefit cheats and scroungers. This shift in focus has real consequences, particularly in relation to rising levels of hate crime against people with a disability.

Recent UK media coverage has focused on welfare changes and the move from Disability Living Allowance (DLA) to Personal Independence Payments. This coverage has been accompanied by some stories about people who have been re-assessed as 'fit for work' (and thus been denied benefits), dying within weeks of their re-assessments and even of disabled people committing suicide when forced to face the reality of living with no money. But alongside these stories are a raft of other pieces about benefit scroungers making fraudulent claims that cheat all the hard-working taxpayers. Carry out a search on the term 'disability' in a well-known tabloid newspaper and you find two pages of headlines on the benefits that are 'handed out to addicts and alcoholics', the 'breakdancers', 'traffic wardens' and 'holidaying conwomen' fraudulently claiming DLA, and the £1 billion that could be reclaimed if the half of claimants who are fraudsters were forced back to work.

The message is clear. People on DLA are benefits scroungers who should be out looking for work. This is exacerbated by comments from the newly appointed MP for Disabled People, Esther McVey, who, in an interview on Channel 4, suggested that DLA is a dynamic benefit, that bodies heal and that a third of disabled people will get better and no longer need the benefits that they are receiving. And yet the Government's own figures, derived from spot checks carried out by the Department for Work and Pensions suggests that only 0.5% of DLA claims are fraudulent and that more people are actually underpaid than overpaid.

In his work on the politics of disablement, Mike Oliver highlighted the importance of thinking about how we defined disability and disabled people. He suggested that definitions are important because we orientate our behaviour towards people according to how we define them. If we see disabled people as tragic victims then we seek to 'care' for them. If we see them as oppressed then we fight for their rights. And if we see them as scroungers and cheats then we hate. He goes on to say that definitions provide a social classification – identifying

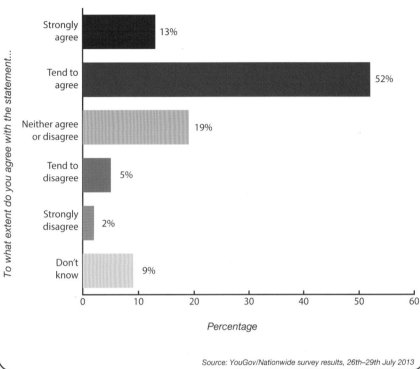

To what extent do you agree or disagree with the statement that 'Since the London 2012 Paralympic Games, disabled people are recognised more than ever as being able to lead normal lives and achieve great things'

Source: YouGov/Nationwide survey results, 26th–29th July 2013

people as unwilling or unable to work. The DLA can be seen as a label which reflects the fact that a person may incur extra costs carrying out everyday tasks – hence a legitimation of need. And yet this is being challenged through Government and media campaigns focussing on the very small number of fraudulent claims, the small minority who recover from temporary disabilities, and ignoring the very real fear amongst disabled people who face potentially losing their benefits and their independence. And the result is a rise in hate crime.

Statistics presented by Tom Shakespeare at the UK Disability Studies Conference in 2012 suggest that disabled adults are 50% more likely to be victims of crime than non-disabled adults. Adults with mental health issues are four times more likely to be victims of violent crime and ten times more likely to be victims of hate crime than their non-disabled peers. Furthermore, disabled children are 57% more likely to be bullied and children

with learning difficulties are four times more likely to be bullied or abused. Not only are disabled people more likely to be victims of hate crime than non-disabled people, the numbers over hate crimes reported over the past two years are going up.

The rise in hate crime reflects the media representation of disabled people as scroungers and cheats, providing a convenient backdrop that allows society to passively watch whilst the Government destroys not just the welfare system designed to support those who need help but also the sense of community that underlies it.

31 May 2013

⇨ The above information is reprinted with kind permission from Cost Of Living. Please visit www.cost-ofliving.net for further information.

New research exposes the lack of real participation opportunities for disabled young people

Disabled young people are being denied the right to have a say in how local services, such as education, health and leisure are being developed and delivered, reveals new research released today.

The VIPER research, carried out by a group of 16 disabled young people, looked at their participation and involvement in decision-making and the barriers that prevent them from having a say.

The young researchers worked in partnership with the Alliance for Inclusive Education (ALLFIE), the Children's Society, the Council for Disabled Children and the National Children's Bureau Research Centre.

Their findings highlight how disabled young people are systematically excluded from sharing their views on the services they rely on and use every day. This is despite numerous initiatives to promote disabled children and young people's participation in local decision-making. Many of the young disabled people involved in the research feel local participation opportunities are, at best, tokenistic.

Rebecca, a young disabled VIPER researcher, said: 'If more services took account of young disabled people's views in decision-making we would have better and more effective services. Currently young disabled people are not having the opportunity to have their say and this needs to change.'

The young VIPER researchers have produced a set of recommendations for Government and local services. The aim is to challenge the lack of support for disabled young people's participation in decision-making. To ensure that young disabled people's opinions are at the centre of developing and delivering local services, the recommendations include:

⇨ Giving disabled young people's participation a clear mandate in the Children and Families Bill, placing it at the centre of the special educational needs and disability (SEND) reforms.

⇨ Involving disabled young people in decisions about services from the very beginning, not once decisions are already made.

⇨ Asking central Government to promote how services can use existing laws and guidance to support disabled young people's participation, for example the Equality Act Public Sector Equality Duty, UN Convention on the Rights of the Child, and UN Convention on the Rights of Persons with Disabilities.

Tara Flood, Director of ALLFIE said: 'It is clear from the VIPER research findings that there is still some real resistance from service providers to listening to young disabled people in terms of what support they want. We hope the recommendations will persuade providers to see the value in including young disabled people in decision-making.'

Notes

1. 'VIPER' stands for Voice, Inclusion, Participation, Empowerment and Research. A group of 16 young disabled people work as joint researchers on this project and chose the name for the project to describe what they want to achieve for other disabled young people. The 'Vipers' are a diverse group in age, impairment group, location and background with few having any research experience before this project. They met regularly to undertake bespoke research training; participated in every stage of the research, and made decisions about every stage of the project, including prioritising recommendations for change.

2. The research was carried out using a range of methods including a literature review; an online survey of organisations working with disabled children and young people; and a series of interviews with young disabled people, project workers and strategic managers in eight local authorities in England. The research took place between July 2010 and September 2012.

3. The research findings indicate that:

⇨ Many disabled young people are still being excluded from decision-making opportunities

⇨ Disabled young people's participation is not fully embedded in decisions about their care and support; how services run; or how services are designed and commissioned

⇨ Disabled young people's access needs are often not being met. This prevents them from being able to take part in decision-making opportunities

⇨ There is a lack of feedback and understanding of the positive impact of disabled young people's participation in decision-making.

⇨ This research consisted of a survey of 204 organisations, 28 interviews with project staff and senior managers, eight focus groups with disabled young people and an online survey of schools in one local authority.

4. The VIPER full research findings and reports can be downloaded at http://www.councilfordisabledchildren.org.uk/viper.

5. The VIPER report *Hear Us Out* featuring key findings and recommendations based on the research findings can be downloaded at http://www.councilfordisabledchildren.org.uk/viper.

6. VIPER is a three-year project funded by the Big Lottery, and delivered in partnership by the National Children's Bureau Research Centre, the Alliance for Inclusive Education, the Council for Disabled Children and The Children's Society.

The project is part of the Big Lottery Fund research programme.

7. In this project we are specifically researching disabled young people's participation in decisions about service development. We also mean that 'participation' is a process where groups or individuals can influence decision-making and bring about change.

8. More information about the government's SEND reform proposals and the Education Select Committees recommendations can be found at http://www.education.gov.uk/childrenandyoungpeople/send/changingsen

5 February 2013

⇨ The above information is reprinted with kind permission from the National Children's Bureau. Please visit www.ncb.org.uk for further information.

© National Children's Bureau 2013

People with learning disabilities need more choice over where they live

A new initiative aims to offer people affordable housing close to their family and friends by simplifying tenancy arrangements.

By Duncan Cameron and Alicia Wood

Getting housing is tough for many people in Britain today. Young people stay in the family home longer because they can't get mortgages, private rented housing is expensive and sometimes poor quality, and investment in social housing has shrunk.

People with learning disabilities struggle more than most to get decent housing. Although most people want a home of their own in their own communities, they are often forced to accept places in residential services where they cannot choose their flatmates or how they get support. A bad situation has been made even worse by housing shortages, reduced benefit entitlements and significant cuts in social care.

More social housing would help, but it may not be the only solution. The Cameron Trust, Housing and Support Alliance and the Centre for Welfare Reform have launched the 'Investing in Ordinary Lives' initiative to explore how private finance could be used to develop ethical housing options for people with learning disabilities.

Many in social housing are suspicious of private investment, and not without reason. Most of it goes into residential care homes or short-term mortgages that demand rents so high they are neither ethical nor sustainable.

However, for people with learning disabilities who just need an ordinary home, the supported housing available from the not-for-profit sector is also often unaffordable. Much of the funding for it seems to be lost in organisational overheads. Perhaps some of those costs can be justified but unless people need adapted or specially designed housing, rent for a supported house should not be any higher than similar housing in the same area. The special systems designed with good intentions often seem to create additional costs, bureaucracy and hurdles for people with disabilities.

Perhaps we can develop better housing solutions by bringing together the public, private and voluntary sectors to focus on what disabled people really want: how do we get people housing that keeps them close to their friends and family? How do we give people control over how they live and how they are supported? How do we do this in the most affordable and sustainable way possible?

The Cameron Trust has developed a model where landlords, wealthy individuals and investors can invest in properties to give people with learning disabilities ten-year tenancies based on their preferences. We need to move closer to the private rental models in Europe where tenancies are for longer periods and are much more secure.

Investors need reasonable and secure returns on their investment and it turns out they can get them.

Most of the properties managed by the Cameron Trust charge rents that match the Local Housing Allowance even where there have been major adaptations. Overheads are kept low by bringing the landlord and tenant as close together as possible and minimising bureaucracy. Housing and Support Alliance match the tenant with landlords and we can draw on a range of landlords and different funding sources.

Perhaps until now we have over-complicated what should be a very simple transaction. There are people who need places to live that the state must pay for, and there are people and organisations who have the money to buy and rent housing to those people at reasonable rents with security. Why should we spend public money on housing and care models that people don't want when we can spend it on what they do want? Let's just get on with it.

Duncan Cameron is founder of the Cameron Trust and co-founder of moneysupermarket.com. Alicia Wood is chief executive of the Housing and Support Alliance

2 July 2013

⇨ The above information is reprinted with kind permission from *The Guardian*. Please visit www.guardian.co.uk for further information.

Doing Sport Differently

A guide to exercise and fitness for people living with disability or health conditions.

Why do sport?

Doing Sport Differently is not just for the next Tanni Grey-Thompson. It's not even for the few who have ever played competitive sport at any level. It's for everyone. When we talk about sport, exercise and physical activity, we're talking about things that everyone can do – disabled and non-disabled alike. It needn't be competitive, it needn't be hard work, it just needs to be fun.

If you want to be more physically active but don't know how, this is the guide for you. Even if you think you hate sport and don't believe that taking more exercise is beneficial or even possible for you, read on – you may be surprised.

With London hosting the 2012 Olympic and Paralympic Games, the idea of sport for all has never been higher on the agenda. For people who want to get active, there have never been more opportunities than now. You don't even need to leave the house.

I can't get fit and healthy, I'm disabled

Disability is created by the environment not by you, your impairment or health condition. If you're a wheelchair-user stuck outside a building without a ramp, what is the barrier? The injury that makes it easier for you to use a chair or the lack of a ramp? Add a ramp and not only can you access the building more easily but so can older people, people with prams, people with heavy luggage, children – pretty much everyone in fact. It's the absence of the ramp that is disabling.

The same applies to sport. Again, to take a wheelchair-user as an example, there's nothing stopping you rolling your wheelchair onto the nearest tennis court and having a go except the rules of the club or the width of the gate onto the court or the attitudes of the other players. Nothing that can't be changed.

But wheelchairs are just an example. This applies in different ways to all of us experiencing disability or a health condition. The barriers to someone with a mental health condition or a learning difficulty doing sport may be less obvious than a flight of stairs but they're there all the same in the attitudes, organisation and environment around exercise.

Of course, your impairment or health condition may affect what you can do. But whatever your impairment or health condition, you are you and taking some exercise will make you a fitter, healthier you.

Health and fitness, of course, are not the same thing either.

Fitness is largely physical. It's about your capacity to deal with the environment around you so

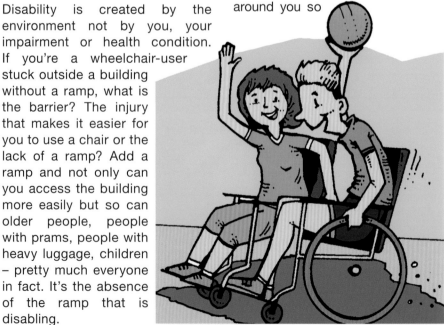

a fitter wheelchair-user may be able to wheel him or herself further and faster.

Health is about more than this. It includes physical, mental and social well-being. This involves self-acceptance. The well-known serenity prayer puts its finger on it very well and you don't need to be religious to get it. It wishes for us the serenity to accept the things we cannot change, the courage to change the things we can, and the wisdom to know the difference. This is something we all need to understand to be healthy, especially if we're doing sport or exercise.

And that brings us right back to disability because one of the things that we can change is the disabling environment of barriers and attitudes.

The law is there to help us do this. Under the Equality Act 2010 (which is based on the disability discrimination legislation that went before it), it is unlawful for service providers to treat disabled people less favourably because they are disabled. Service providers must make 'reasonable adjustments' to the way they provide their services to remove the barriers preventing disabled people from accessing them. This applies to the local gym or football stadium as much as it does to banks, pubs or cinemas.

'Reasonable' refers to the resources available for adjustments so a service provider can only avoid making them if he or she can show that it would be genuinely too impractical, too disruptive or too expensive to do so.

So what does all this mean in practice? It means simply this: anyone can get fitter and healthier regardless of their impairment or health condition – mental health condition, learning difficulty, physical impairment, whatever.

2 July 2013

⇨ The above information is reprinted with kind permission from Disability Rights UK. Please visit www.disabilityrightsuk.org for further information.

Disabled people say Paralympics have improved public attitudes

The majority of disabled people think that the 2012 Paralympic Games in London have had a positive impact on attitudes.

But the new poll from the disability charity Scope – the first to ask disabled people what they think of the Paralympics effect – also shows that many disabled people still experience discrimination on a regular basis.

The charity's Chief Executive Richard Hawkes says that the poll shows that the Paralympics effect is real.

But he argues you don't change attitudes in a fortnight, and charities, the media and the Government must now build on the momentum.

Paralympics poll

72% of disabled people think that the Paralympics have had a positive impact on attitudes. 20% say it's changed the way people talk to them and 20% say it's made people more aware of their needs.

However, 54% say they experience discrimination on a regular basis, with 84% of disabled people saying people patronise them and 63.5% saying they have experienced people refusing to make adjustments or do things differently.

The poll is a follow-up to a survey conducted by Scope before the Paralympics. In that survey, disabled people claimed that attitudes were getting worse, but also that the Paralympics (through greater visibility and more discussions) could make a difference.

The 'Paralympics effect'

The poll comes as the debate continues over the so-called Paralympics effect.

In September, Lord Coe's view that 'we would never look at disability in the same way again' was backed up by polling from Channel 4.

However, in October, disabled people took to the streets to protest against cuts.

A series of reports underlined the impact of spiralling living costs, stagnant incomes and the loss of national and local support on the lives of disabled people and their families.

Baroness Tanni Grey-Thompson, speaking to a national newspaper, asked where the evidence is of a change in attitudes.

Don't write-off the Paralympics effect

But according to Richard Hawkes we shouldn't write off the Paralympics effect. He said: 'Disabled people tell Scope that greater visibility and public discussion of their lives makes a difference.

'During the Games, Ellie Simmonds, David Weir and Jonnie Peacock became national heroes. Disability was consistently, openly and widely talked about like never before. Channel 4's poll taken straight after the Games pointed to a change in public attitudes.

'But it takes longer than a fortnight to change attitudes. Times are undoubtedly tough for disabled people. But maybe rather than write the Paralympics effect off, we should be asking what we can do to build on it and keep it going.

'The Paralympics in London happens once in a lifetime. But let's ask what else we can do increase disabled people's visibility in the media, in politics, in the arts and above all in everyday life?

'At Scope – through our work on the ground, through our campaigns – we aim to make this a better place for disabled people. But is there more that we and other charities can do?

'Channel 4 is investing in disabled talent. Other broadcasters have schemes in place, but is there more we can do to get disabled talent into the mainstream?

'Esther McVey, Minister for Disabled People, has said we need to build on the Paralympics legacy.

'Can she explain to her colleagues that benefits shouldn't be a dirty word? Every Paralympic athlete will have had some support to overcome the barriers. The starting point for welfare should be what do disabled people need to live their lives – not what can we take away to save money?'

Views of disabled people

Ade Adepitan MBE – Scope patron, TV presenter and former Paralympic wheelchair basketball player, said:

'London 2012 helped generate some bright disabled role models who can really make a difference to the perceptions of the public for many years to come. I think the Paralympics will create a lot of opportunities but there's a job to do now to build on this and get more disabled people visible in the mainstream.'

Rhona Kingett, from Leicester, is in her mid-40s and has multiple sclerosis. She said: 'On a small scale and in local areas I think attitudes have changed for the better. However, the bigger issues in society relating to disability still need to be addressed and tackled.'

Sarah Kiley, from Greater Manchester, has a son Philip, who is aged eight and has Down's Syndrome. She said: 'I am not sure if the Paralympics had a big effect on attitudes in society, but it has had an impact on me personally. I feel like I can now go forward with more confidence and more power to question or challenge attitudes.'

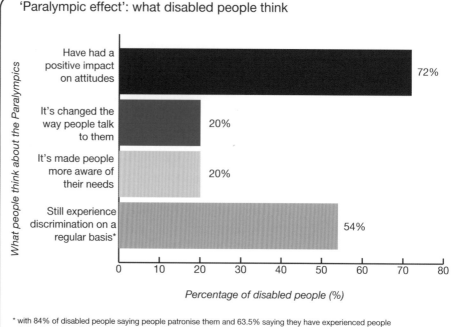

'Paralympic effect': what disabled people think

What people think about the Paralympics

- Have had a positive impact on attitudes — 72%
- It's changed the way people talk to them — 20%
- It's made people more aware of their needs — 20%
- Still experience discrimination on a regular basis* — 54%

Percentage of disabled people (%)

* with 84% of disabled people saying people patronise them and 63.5% saying they have experienced people refusing to make adjustments or do things differently.

Source: Paralympic Poll, Scope, 2013. © Scope 2013

Ian Macrae, editor of *Disability Now*, said: 'Some things have changed. The profile of disability sport is much, much higher and Paralympic events and achievements are taken more seriously. The fact that there are three Paralympians on the shortlist for BBC Sports Personality of the Year is indicative of this. There's also been a certain amount of change in the general perception of disability. But I don't think any of this has had much of an impact on the lives of the vast majority of disabled people. We are still facing endemic and institutionalised discrimination and denial of rights, opportunities and equality. More of us live in poverty than in society as a whole. Affordable accessible housing is scarce. Many disabled children are being poorly served by an education system not geared up to meet their needs. We have less access to employment. Getting around is generally more difficult and often more expensive. All of this means that many of us feel isolated and apart from the communities of which we should be a fully integrated part.'

Martyn Sibley, co-founder of disability lifestyle website Disability Horizons, said:

'I can say I think attitudes have changed for the better but we need to turn this goodwill into improved transport, public building and employment for disabled people. There's still a lot to do.'

13 December 2012

⇨ The above information is reprinted with kind permission from Scope. Please visit www.scope.org for further information.

'Paralympics hasn't improved daily lives for disabled'

By James Nadal

The Paralympics has not helped improve the daily lives of disabled people, a leading Bucks campaign group says.

The event has been hailed as shifting public attitudes towards disability but Wycombe Area Access for All said while the achievements of Paralympic athletes were brilliant, the games have not led to significant changes to help the disabled in everyday life.

The organisation, representing people with disabilities in High Wycombe, Marlow and across the Wycombe district, said public transport in the area, in particular, remains a major problem.

Travelling to hospital, particularly now with services moving to Stoke Mandeville from Wycombe, has been highlighted as particularly hard.

The experience of shopping in a town centre like Marlow, especially the basics of getting inside a store without help, has not changed, WAAFA said.

Significant improvements have not happened despite the profile of Paralympians at London 2012 – and also Wycombe District Council's pledge to make the area the most disabled friendly nationwide – the pressure group said.

WAAFA told the Free Press: 'Has the Paralympics meant we can get a bus to Stoke Mandeville? Has that meant the nitty gritty infrastructure is left in a better state?

'No, it hasn't. The Paralympics hasn't changed that.'

Too many shops in towns around Wycombe still do not have ramps or wheelchair access and the internal layout is often difficult to navigate in a chair or a scooter, the organisation said.

The height of counters, for example at banks, or self-service check-outs at supermarkets, are also an issue, as are things such as switches for doors and electronic passes, WAAFA said.

It said: 'It's all the little things that come together, it's the whole combination. We don't want wrapping in cotton wool, we don't want that. It's just about when we get into the bank for example, we want to be able to access the counter.

'It's not just the disability that disables us, it's society.'

The organisation said people in wheelchairs just want to be able to get into a shop on their own without the embarrassment and inconvenience of having to be lifted in.

Buses, trains and other public transport continues to be a major concern.

'Public transport is not yet effective (in the Wycombe district) and not as effective as they (authorities) would like to think that it is,' the group said.

For example, disabled people living in Marlow can not get directly to Bourne End or Beaconsfield by bus, the organisation pointed out.

A taxi fitted out to carry disabled passengers, from Marlow to High Wycombe, costs about £50 return and buses which say they are wheelchair friendly often are not, with ramps not in use, it added.

The council's Improvement and Review Commission will examine progress in the targets it set out last year to make it the most disabled friendly in the UK in September.

14 August 2013

⇨ The above information is reprinted with kind permission from Newsquest Media Group and originally appeared in the *Bucks Free Press*. Please visit www.bucksfreepress.co.uk for further information.

What is a Recognised Assistance Dog?

What is a Recognised Assistance Dog?

A 'Recognised Assistance Dog' is one which has been specifically trained to assist a disabled person and which has been qualified by one of the charitable organisations registered as members of Assistance Dogs UK. Assistance dogs trained by members of Assistance Dogs UK will have formal identification and have been endorsed by the Department of Health, on the basis that the dog's high standards of training, behaviour, health and welfare are such that it should be permitted to accompany its client, owner or partner, at all times and in all places, within the United Kingdom.

Assistance dogs from other nations, when entering the UK, should meet the full membership criteria of the established international assistance dog organisations – Assistance Dogs International, Assistance Dogs Europe, International Guide Dog Federation – or other such international bodies as may from time to time be recognised.

Currently the following organisations are registered Full Members of Assistance Dogs UK:

⇨ Canine Partners

⇨ Dog A.I.D.

⇨ Dogs for the Disabled

⇨ Hearing Dogs for Deaf People

⇨ Support Dogs

⇨ Guide Dogs

⇨ Medical Detection Dogs.

How do I know that the person who is accompanied by a Recognised Assistance Dog has a disability and would therefore be covered by the Equality Act?

People with disabilities have the right not to face discrimination under the Equality Act 2010. Full information is available from the Equality and Human Rights Commission. If somebody has qualified to be partnered with a Registered Assistance Dog they will have had to show clear evidence of their disability by means of medical assessments and reports. Some disabilities may not be visible.

Why should I allow a disabled person to be accompanied by their Recognised Assistance Dog?

The Equality Act says that reasonable adjustments must be made in order to avoid discriminating against people with disabilities. These will range from creating an access route for a person with a wheelchair to waiving a 'no dogs policy' in order that a disabled person may be accompanied by their Recognised Assistance Dog. All Recognised Assistance Dogs perform practical assistive tasks for their disabled partners to avoid them being at a disadvantage and to enable them to be independent, or provide guiding skills in the case of blind or partially sighted people – for this reason it is reasonable to allow Recognised Assistance Dogs to accompany their partners into situations where pet dogs would not be permitted.

Surely, Assistance Dogs are a health hazard?

Assistance Dogs UK acknowledges that it would not be reasonable for any dog to be allowed access into somewhere with a 'no dogs policy' if it were to constitute a risk to anybody's Health or Safety. For this reason all Recognised Assistance Dogs receive special training and healthcare and are tested on a regular basis to ensure that they do not present any risks.

How can you be sure a Recognised Assistance Dog won't bite anyone?

All Recognised Assistance Dogs are selected by experts in order to ensure their trustworthy temperament. They are continually assessed in a variety of situations over a period of several months before they are considered ready to be qualified. It would not be possible to guarantee the temperament of dogs if this long, careful assessment process were not undertaken over several months.

How can you be sure a Recognised Assistance Dog won't put anyone's safety at risk because of their behaviour?

All Recognised Assistance Dogs are trained by expert dog-trainers over a period of several months in order to ensure that they are entirely under control at all times and that they won't constitute any sort of risk or nuisance to anyone. For example, Recognised Assistance Dogs are trained to lie quietly under the table when their partner is eating at a restaurant. Their standards are assessed in a variety of situations over a period of several months before they are considered ready to be qualified. All Recognised Assistance Dogs must pass various tests and these include tests relating not only to their standards of obedience but also proving that the dogs do perform the practical assistive tasks that their partner requires. It would not be possible to guarantee the behaviour and training of dogs if this long, careful training and assessment process were not undertaken over several months and in a variety of different environments.

How can you be sure a recognised Assistance Dog won't put anyone's health at risk because of canine illnesses or health conditions that might be passed to people?

Assistance Dogs UK acknowledges that in order to prevent any risk to people's health, all Recognised Assistance Dogs must be regularly vaccinated, wormed and de-flead in accordance with the very latest veterinary advice, using the very best products. Not only this, but all Recognised Assistance Dogs also receive regular health assessments by vets. Assistance Dogs UK can only guarantee that Recognised Assistance Dogs receive this regular healthcare by ensuring that partners of dogs provide on-going evidence of these healthcare treatments several times a year. Less-frequent or less-comprehensive checks would not suffice. For example, annual evidence of healthcare would not be sufficient to guarantee freedom from parasites throughout the year.

How can you be sure that the disabled partner is able to handle their dog and ensure its healthcare, in the same way as the dog's expert trainer?

Assistance Dogs UK requires that the disabled people who are partnered with Recognised Assistance Dogs must receive comprehensive training (generally at least 18 days supervised by a professional trainer) in all aspects of dog behaviour, training and welfare in order that they are entirely safe to handle a dog in a variety of situations. No partner passes through the course if they are not deemed to have attained the correct standard. All Recognised Assistance Dogs must pass a Qualification Test during which they are handled entirely by their disabled partner, before qualifying. This test encompasses obedience, both on and off lead, public access behaviour, specific assistive tasks and understanding of dog welfare and health.

How can you be sure a Recognised Assistance Dog won't cause a problem to people who are allergic to dogs?

The Equality Act 2010 requires that disabled people have the same rights to services such as accommodation, restaurants, pubs and cafes as everyone else. It includes a duty to make reasonable adjustments to ensure that disabled people can access services. This includes amending a 'no dogs' policy to allow guide and assistance dogs.

Allergy to dogs is sometimes given as a reason to not admit guide and assistance dogs. While the prevalence of allergies generally is increasing worldwide and it is of course not an issue to be taken lightly, the incidence of allergies to dogs may be less than perhaps commonly thought. In the UK, approximately 8% of adults are sensitive to dog allergens, while it is estimated that up to four times as many people are allergic to pollen and house dust mites. Where a clear allergy risk to a specific individual can be objectively identified by an establishment, steps should be taken to reduce this risk, but refusal of access for guide and assistance dogs based on the possibility that other people 'may' be allergic is unlikely to be classed as a reasonable or proportionate response.

How can you guarantee that Recognised Assistance Dogs maintain the same high standards of behaviour for the whole of their working life, regardless of whether their disabled partner's circumstances change?

Assistance Dogs UK stresses the absolute importance of providing regular aftercare support to all Recognised Assistance Dogs partnerships. All recognised partnerships are re-assessed at least once a year as an absolute minimum. Without such regular aftercare, no guarantees could be provided regarding the ongoing standards of the partnerships.

What if a problem suddenly arises with a Recognised Assistance Dog or its partner which means that the standards of the partnership fall?

All members of Assistance Dogs UK agree to control the standards of all their Recognised Assistance Dogs at all times. As soon as any problem were to arise, resulting in a drop in standards, whether due to a change of circumstances in either the dog or the human partner, the organisation that trained the partnership would take immediate action to address the situation. Partnerships only maintain their recognised status if the necessary standards are maintained. This gives complete peace of mind to all concerned. The same peace of mind would not be present if partnerships did not have the same support from organisations.

Can my pet dog be registered as a Recognised Assistance Dog?

You will realise from the answers to the questions above that Recognised Assistance Dogs are highly trained and their temperament is tested over a long training period. It would not be feasible for any 'registration' body to be able to assess a dog effectively without observing it for a long period of time. For this reason, none of the members of Assistance Dogs (UK) provide a registration service for pet dogs. However, Dog A.I.D. do support the training of people's pet dogs which go through a rigorous training programme over many months under the guidance of highly experienced instructors. See Dog A.I.D. website for further information.

I am an assistance dog owner and have been refused access to a public place. What should I do?

Being refused access can be a very humiliating and stressful thing to deal with. A lot of service providers are just not aware of their obligations under the Equality Act 2010 so providing initial information about access rights for assistance dogs is the first step. In many cases, when service providers realise they are at fault they are more than happy to help to resolve the problem. You can point the service provider to the AD(UK) website if they ask for further information. However, if they continue to refuse to deal positively with the issue, it would probably be best to contact your assistance dog organisation and they will support you in any way they can. Where necessary, the organisations that form part of AD(UK) work together to ensure compliance with the law on access rights.

In the UK at the present time, there are no charities that train dogs for people with mental health issues where this is the only disability. Psychiatric Service dogs are trained in some other countries, but not in the UK. This is a very specialist area of work and whilst in time, it is likely that a charity in the UK will offer this service, at present it is not available. Should there be any change in this position, information will be posted on the Assistance Dogs website.

2 July 2013

⇨ The above information is reprinted with kind permission from Assistance Dogs. Please visit www.assistancedogs.org.uk for further information.

Thousands of children as young as five act as family carers, figures show

More than 177,000 minors look after relatives, with charities warning long hours affect schoolwork and childhood.

By Ben Quinn

Nearly 10,000 children aged five to seven are acting as unpaid carers for family members or guardians, according to figures that have been published which were described by one children's charity as the tip of the iceberg.

The data, compiled from the 2011 Census, shows nearly a quarter of a million people under 19 in England and Wales were caring for parents, siblings and others – coping with pressures which charities say cause many to fall behind in school and miss out on their own childhoods.

An 80% increase in the number of five- to seven-year-old carers in England over the last decade was one of the starker trends to emerge, although observers suggest this may be because the size of this group was under-reported in the past.

Girls are slightly more likely to be carers than boys, while youngsters from black, Asian or other minority ethnic communities were twice as likely to be carers. The Children's Society said that the figures were unlikely to represent the true picture as many child carers remain hidden from the view of authorities.

The charity called for greater state support for young carers, who it said were one and a half times more likely to have a long-standing illness or disability or special educational need than their peers. They also have significantly lower educational attainment at GCSE level – the equivalent of nine grades lower overall than their peers.

'Many young carers remain hidden from official sight for a host of reasons, including family loyalty, stigma, bullying, not knowing where to go for support,' the charity said in a report, *Hidden From View*, which pointed out that the number of young carers in England had risen by a fifth since the last census in 2001.

The latest Census figures reveal that a total of 177,918 minors are carers for their loved ones, with 15,728 providing more than 50 hours of care a week and 19,422 between 20 and 49 hours. Children aged ten to 14 made up the largest group of young care providers, with 72,266 providing unpaid care.

Of the 9,985 five- to seven-year-olds providing care, 1,642 are doing so for more than 50 hours a week, and 1,166 for between 20 and 49 hours. In the eight- to nine-year-old age bracket, 12,148 children are giving care, 1,520 for more than 50 hours a week and 1,204 for between 20 and 49 hours. Statistics on the levels of health among child carers revealed that more than 2,400 had bad or very bad health, while more than 9,000 said it was 'fair'.

Matthew Reed, chief executive of The Children's Society, said: 'This new figure is shocking enough, but we know from years of working with young carers that it is likely to be just the tip of the iceberg. Many often incredibly vulnerable young carers are slipping through the net, undetected by the support services they so desperately need.'

David Holmes, chief executive of Family Action, which supports disadvantaged and socially isolated families, said it wanted the Government to address the needs of young carers through the Children and Families Bill currently before Parliament. 'We would like to see a duty on schools to identify young carers in the school population and the development of improved support,' said Holmes, who added that many young carers felt unable to disclose their caring responsibilities because of a lack of trust in teachers or a fear of agencies intervening at home or worries about being bullied.

A Department for Education spokeswoman said: 'We know young carers need more help and we are supporting local authorities to do much more for these dedicated young people. 'We recently announced that young carers will be involved in the training of school nurses, so they know exactly what support they should offer and can champion their needs.

'We have also created a specific training guide for teachers to help them to better identify and support young carers – and funded The Children's Society and Carers Trust to support social services to adopt "whole family" approaches to support young carers.'

Case study: 'I had to grow up'

For Jack Garrigan, the moment he had to very quickly start taking on adult responsibilities came last year when his mother, Louise, lost her sight after the sudden onset of a rare virus.

'Mum was in hospital for a month and it was over four weeks that I had to grow up really,' says the 15-year-old, who, along with his sister Laura, ten, is among nearly a quarter of a million children in England and Wales caring for a relative.

In the case of the Garrigan family, from the Blackley district of Manchester, it involves Jack stepping in to cook, shop and, in his mother's words, ensure the household keeps running.

'The three of us work as a team, so we all do our bit,' he says. 'On a typical morning, for example, my sister would help my mum get dressed and I would prepare the breakfast and make sure that Laura is looking nice for school too.'

The routine takes its toll – 'Sometimes you can get tired, especially when there are school exams going on as well' – and he admits to missing some things that other 15-year-olds enjoy. 'I used to go to a drama club workshop but I can't do it any longer because there is no way of getting there and I have too much to do,' he says.

But he adds matter-of-factly: 'At the end of the day she is my mum and whatever I do, I do it because I have to and because I want to.'

Concerned that her son is playing down his role in the family, Mrs Garrigan adds: 'I don't think he really knows how much he does because it's so constant and we are in a routine now. He does my tablets and prescriptions. He basically keeps the house going.'

16 May 2013

⇨ The above information is reprinted with kind permission from *The Guardian*. Please visit www.guardian.co.uk for further information.

What is caring?

Every day 6,000 people take on a new caring role in the UK. Up and down the UK there are 6.5 million people caring unpaid for an ill, frail or disabled family member or friend. These people are called carers but they would probably say 'I'm just being a husband, a wife, a mum, a dad, a son, a daughter, a friend or a good neighbour.'

When people need help with their day-to-day living they often turn to their family and friends. Looking after each other is something that we do. We should all be prepared to care.

Carers help with personal things: getting someone washed and dressed, turning them in their sleep, helping them move about or administering their medication. Carers also help with things like shopping, laundry, cleaning, cooking, filling in forms or managing money.

Carers Week celebrates and recognises the contribution of all of the UK's 6.5 million unpaid carers.

What do carers do?

Carers:

⇨ Administer medication

⇨ Offer practical support (household tasks, etc.)

⇨ Offer emotional support

⇨ Provide personal care

⇨ Help with financial matters

⇨ Provide physical support/help.

Who do carers care for?

⇨ 40% care for their parent/parents in law

⇨ 26% care for a spouse/partner

⇨ 8% care for disabled children

⇨ 5% care for adult children

⇨ 4% care for grandparents

⇨ 7% care for other relatives

⇨ 9% care for a friend or neighbour.

⇨ The above information is reproduced with kind permission from Carers UK. Please visit www.carersuk.org for further information.

© Carers UK

What happens to older disabled people?

As old age approaches for Ann Young, it's not just her health that worries her. It's a lack of income that concerns her more.

In the disability movement we talk about Choices and Rights but what real choices and rights will I really have as an older disabled person living on the state?

I have tried to work, all my adult life; it hasn't been easy and two redundancies have inflicted some deep scars. But I still believe that work pays in so many ways. It's not just about pride or being financially independent and in control. For me, it's about securing a future for myself and my family where I don't become dependent on them or worse still, the state. I fear getting old in a society that does not seem to value older people, let alone older disabled people. Allan Sutherland, in his brilliant poem, asks 'What Happens to Old Epileptics?' I want to know, what happens to old disabled people? I have met very few older people with my own condition, cerebral palsy – where do we go and how on Earth do we live in our old age if we haven't paid into the system? Are we shut away in our own homes reliant on a crumbling social care system?

My biggest nightmare is to be trapped in an institution; I've been there, done that. Even as a young child, it wasn't a pleasant experience. If we wish to control our own destinies, don't we need an income in order to do that?

Maybe I'm missing a trick – do disabled people on work-related benefits get their National Insurance paid and build up decent pensions? Is that why some can volunteer to work for no pay? Someone please tell me because the way I see it, we are facing a time bomb of increased hardship and poverty as a generation reaches old age with no security, no independence and no choices about how they spend their twilight years.

I except that some disabled people will never be able to compete in the labour market and face a life on benefits due to the nature of their impairment. But I would also argue that our labour market has become so competitive in recent years that people, including myself, have just given up because no matter how capable they are, it is nigh on impossible to compete with the influx of non-disabled people desperately needing work. So what happens to those of us left in the dole queue? Do we not need to earn a living? Is there some magical everlasting safety net just for us?

I can't see that I have any different choices from non-disabled people. I still have a mortgage to pay, a family to provide for and a future to worry about. Luckily I worked for 26 years in good jobs and have managed to secure a small pension while saving a bit to help my son through Higher Education. But I haven't paid 30 years worth of National Insurance contributions so unless I earn for another four years, all the blood, sweat and tears will have been pointless as I approach the end of my life with very little security.

So, what is the answer? For me it was self-employment. I am lucky that there are still a few local disability organisations who believe in me as a professional disabled person. But we need more, many more to believe in disabled people and take a chance of them.

Employment opportunities for disabled people are shrinking. The quota system was abolished in 1995 with the introduction of the DDA and many sheltered work schemes have vanished so isn't it time for user-led organisations (ULOs) to be even more proactive in creating work opportunities for disabled people? It makes sense from a grassroots perspective. I want to receive services from people I trust to know my issues and share my experiences. Isn't that the whole point of grassroots organisations?

If ULOs are really committed to empowering disabled people and reducing poverty, they could use positive discrimination which, if the Internet is correct, is still legal under the DDA. I don't like having to resort to any form of discrimination but in reality, even I recognise that we need something to even out the playing field in the workplace and give disabled people a leg up. I'm tired of hearing the argument that service providers, which many ULOs are these days, owe it to their clients to provide the best service possible and so go for the most experienced and qualified person for the job. Of course, this will often be a non-disabled person who has had access to education, training and knows the job inside out. Or someone who has been a PA to an existing disabled employee, which gives them an unfair advantage. There are loads of highly qualified non-disabled people all clambering for the same few posts. Like women's groups and ethnic minority organisations, we need our grassroots organisations to take affirmative action and employ more disabled people. This has been argued so many times before but I feel we are losing sight of why ULOs are really here! If people working in the disability sector really believed in the mantra of Rights not Charity, they would embrace the practice of providing more paid work for disabled people.

So if any disabled ULO chief executive or director is reading this, just ask yourself how you got where you are today? Was it pure merit or was it also because someone believed in you? Nearly 30 years ago, two young social services managers took a chance on me, a young disabled girl, straight out of college with no work experience whatsoever, just an English degree and an attitude. I owe those two managers so much. That job opened many other doors, gave me confidence and self-respect and started me on a journey that, although difficult at times, continues to give me satisfaction and pride in the things I have achieved. Other disabled people need that chance to learn about work, to gain confidence and experience and real financial independence. I urge ULOs to take a long, hard look at who they are employing and who they use as volunteers. Look at the routes into employment in their own organisations and how disabled people get the experiences they need to gain paid work. Make volunteering opportunities pay

by creating a skilled disabled workforce. It's no longer enough to encourage disabled people to volunteer and feel you are providing real opportunities, our aspirations should be higher than that. We've all heard of the pink pound, we need our own pound and with it the power to politicise, invest in our disabled people and have a real stake in our future. I can't believe that I am alone in feeling strongly about this.

Have you built up enough savings to be financially independent when you are older? What scares you about becoming an older disabled

person. Do you think user-led organisations should be more proactive about helping to secure disabled people's financial futures by providing work opportunities?

31 August 2013

⇨ The above information is reprinted with kind permission from Disability Now and Ann Young. Please visit www.disabilitynow.com for further information.

Thousands struggling to eat, wash or leave their homes

New research exposes the scale of the Government's social care crisis for disabled people: thousands struggling to eat or wash or leave their homes:

⇨ Almost 40% of disabled people receiving social care support are not having their basic needs met, including eating, washing, dressing or getting out of the house.

⇨ To make matters worse, Government proposals risk up to 105,000 disabled people failing to get basic support for their day-to-day lives.

⇨ A £1.2 billion funding gap in social care support for disabled people under the age of 65 has been exposed.

⇨ Five leading disability charities have come together to urge the Government to guarantee vital support for disabled people to end this crisis.

Social care crisis for disabled people

New research published today exposes the true scale of the Government's social care crisis for disabled people, which has left thousands without access to basic care to help them eat, wash properly and leave their homes.

The report *The Other Care Crisis* is published by Scope, Mencap, The National Autistic Society, Sense and Leonard Cheshire Disability. The leading disability charities are concerned that the debate about social care reform has focused on the needs of an ageing population and sidelined the thousands of disabled people under the age of 65 who rely on care in everyday life.

One third of the people who receive social care are disabled, yet Emma from Cambridge says: 'Not getting the support I need has meant my life is on hold. I have no routine, I feel socially isolated, lonely and of no value to society. I'm only 24; I feel 84.'

The charities are urging the Government to put disabled people at the heart of reforms by setting eligibility for state-funded social care at 'moderate needs' in order to guarantee the most vulnerable people in society basic support in their daily lives.

Evidence of social care crisis

The report, the first comprehensive analysis of how the social care crisis affects disabled people, brings together three new pieces of evidence:

⇨ An extensive study of 600 disabled people's experiences

of the social care system shows almost 40% of disabled people currently receiving some social care support are not having basic needs met, including eating properly, washing, dressing or getting out the house.

⇨ Leading academics at the Personal Social Services Research Unit (PSSRU) within the London School of Economics, the same team commissioned by Andrew Dilnot in his review of social care funding, reveal in a new technical report, that up to 105,000 disabled people are at risk of not receiving any basic support for their day-to-day lives as a direct result of the Government's proposals for social care reform.

⇨ The team at LSE also exposes £1.2 billion funding gap when it comes to social care support for disabled people under the age of 65.

The combination of these findings presents clear and compelling evidence of a social care system that is failing disabled people under the age of 65, at a time when Government reforms through the Care and Support Bill, are being scrutinised by a Joint Committee of MPs and Peers.

Cuts to social care budgets

The charities warn of a social care system on the brink of collapse as a result of years of chronic underfunding by successive Governments. They argue that councils are in an impossible position of wanting to provide more support to the growing numbers of disabled people who require care, at a time when they are facing unprecedented cuts to their budgets.

Of the 600 disabled people the charities spoke to:

⇨ Over a third (36%) said they were unable to eat, wash or leave their homes due to underfunding

⇨ 47% of disabled people said a lack of social care support prevented them from taking part in community life

⇨ 34% said it prevented them from working or volunteering

⇨ 53% of disabled people reporting significant anxiety, isolation and deteriorating mental health as a result of not getting the care they needed.

In the Draft Care and Support Bill, the Government committed to introducing a new national eligibility threshold to end the postcode lottery when it comes to determining who qualifies for state-funded social care support, a move supported by the charities. However, as a result, it is widely anticipated that the Government will drastically limit the number of disabled people who will continue to receive this support by setting eligibility at 'substantial needs'.

The analysis undertaken by the team at LSE and commissioned by Scope, reveals for the first time:

⇨ 105,000 disabled people are at risk of not getting the basic support they need to help them eat, get washed and leave their homes if the Government sets eligibility at 'substantial needs'. This figure comprises:

• 36,000 disabled people who have 'moderate needs' and currently receive some care may lose this basic support.

• An additional 69,000 disabled people with 'moderate needs' who are not receiving any basic support, meaning they are likely to struggle with day-to-day life.

The charities urge the Government to address the £1.2 billion funding gap, the equivalent of 0.17% of public spending, into social care support for disabled people and argue that this is the price the Government must pay to guarantee basic support for the most vulnerable people in our society and prevent this crisis from escalating even further.

Richard Hawkes, Chief Executive of disability charity Scope, said: 'This is shocking evidence of a system that has failed disabled people, effectively condemning them to a life without basic dignity and invisible to society. Times are tough for everyone but being able to eat, wash and leave your home is not a luxury. It is absolutely appalling that this is the sad reality of life for thousands of Britain's disabled people. Enough is enough. We cannot bury our heads in the sand any longer and ignore the desperate situation disabled people find themselves in, without help in their day-to-day lives. We need an urgent and long-term solution from the Government to lift disabled people out of a life without basic support for the daily tasks that everyone else takes for granted.'

Mark Goldring, Chief Executive of learning disability charity Mencap said: 'Imagine not being able to eat, wash or dress yourself. It is unforgivable that there are disabled people in England today who aren't given support for these basic needs, because the social care system has failed them. Because of proposed new rules on eligibility, the Government's planned social care reform may well result in 100,000 disabled people not having their basic needs met. The Government cannot ignore this damning evidence and must commit to long-term funding which will support disabled people to live a life with dignity.'

Mark Lever, Chief Executive of The National Autistic Society (NAS) added: 'For less than 0.2% of public expenditure the Government could ensure that over 100,000 vulnerable people have access to support that meets their basic human needs. Failing to provide this care for adults with autism can have a profound and sometimes devastating effect, resulting in people developing more serious mental health problems that will ultimately be at greater cost to the public purse. The social and communication difficulties that people with autism face are often misunderstood by social care assessors, leading to people with the condition being deemed ineligible for support. It is therefore vital that the Government also ensures that all assessors are trained in autism. Where this does not happen there is a real danger that people will miss out on essential care and consequently find themselves living lives of hardship and misery.'

'Supporting disabled people with moderate needs can prevent those needs from escalating. It may sound like we are calling for a lot of money, but if it helps keep people in work and out of hospital it could make savings to the public purse over time,' said Sir Paul Ennals, Director of Strategy for deafblind charity Sense.

Clare Pelham, Chief Executive of Leonard Cheshire Disability, added: 'There should be no "take it or leave it" mentality in providing care for disabled people. When money is tight, it should go to those who need it most. No-one in this day and age should be left without the help they need to take a bath or dress in the morning, and live an everyday life just like everyone else. This new research reveals for the first time how many people are living in the care "gap" and it is a disgrace. No Government and no right-thinking person should allow this to continue in their street, their town, their country.'

17 January 2013

⇨ The above information is reprinted with kind permission from Scope. Please visit www.scope.org for further information.

© Scope 2013

Dealing with stigma as the parent of a child with disabilities

By Kate Richardson and Rorie Fulton

Having a child with disabilities in the family

The family of a child with disabilities is, first and foremost, a family. Such a family enjoys doing the same simple things that all families enjoy doing – going for a walk in the park, going to the shops, going out for a meal, having friends round. Equally, the parents of a child with disabilities are, first and foremost, parents. They have high hopes and great dreams for their child. They identify and celebrate the same positive qualities in their child – trying hard, keeping on trying, doing their best – as all parents do. Indeed, children with disabilities do try hard, do keep on trying, do try their best, precisely because, first and foremost, they are children. This deep and enduring commonality of experience – between and among all families, all parents, all children – is amply demonstrated in a recent report, *Our family, our future*, in which a number of families with children with disabilities were invited to tell their stories.[1] The following excerpt from the testimony of the parents of 15-year-old Susie-Jo, who has multiple disabilities, is not untypical: 'we are celebrating because our teenage daughter recently held an ice cream and ate the entire thing unaided, thrilled because she's putting her own shoes on, even if she may never do them up by herself'.[2]

Just as each of us shares in this commonality of experience, whether as a son or daughter, mother or father, so each of us may, at any time in our lives, be exposed to conditions which result in a disability. It might be expected that this commonality of experience on the one hand, and shared vulnerability to impairment, on the other, might predispose those of us who have no additional needs to an attitude of empathy and understanding towards those who do. That is to say, it might be expected that our shared humanity might make us respond positively and supportively to children with disabilities and their families when we encounter them in our daily lives. However, sadly, much, if not most of the evidence points in the opposite direction. Too often, these families are thwarted in their attempts at even the most mundane of activities by the prejudice and lack of understanding they encounter when they are out and about. Too often, the attitudes and actions of the general public are unthinkingly negative, even hostile, effectively stigmatising the child with disabilities and, by association, their parents.

Public perceptions of disability

A recent survey of more than 600 parents who care for a child with disabilities found that almost 70% of respondents felt that public understanding and acceptance of disability is poor or unsatisfactory.[3] The same survey identified public attitudes towards disability as one of the three major barriers standing in the way of families of a child with disabilities leading ordinary lives. Negative public attitudes manifest themselves in a number of ways in the lives of parents of a child with disabilities. The Contact a Family survey found that many of the respondents' comments were about 'having to deal with people's stares and comments'.[4] Sadly, this echoes the findings of some of the very earliest academic research into the experience of parents of a child with disabilities, indeed 'the problem of negotiating public encounters is a common theme in most research on stigma'.[5]

Stigma attaches to a child with disabilities and, by association, to their parents.[6] Stigma is fundamentally different from discrimination. Stigma is society's negative evaluation of particular attributes or behaviours.[7] Discrimination, on the other hand, occurs when actions are taken (or not taken) on the basis of a stigmatising belief or assumption. The term 'discrimination' directs our attention at the discriminators, at those who actively reject and exclude, whilst stigma, conversely, focuses attention on those who are rejected and excluded.[8] There is, thus, a diffuse, and difficult to pin down sense that those who experience stigma are somehow themselves responsible for their stigmatised status, a sense in which the stigmatic embodies their own stigma and so cannot escape it.

The stories collected in *Our family, our future*, whilst leavened by much strength, hope and optimism, are coloured more by the difficulties and challenges which the parents of children with disabilities face. Noah is five years old and has severe disabilities. His mother relates that;

'Noah attended a nursery last year, which had a policy of including disabled children. However, he came home with dirty and ripped trousers after his first day and when I called to ask if everything was OK, they said they couldn't cope with

1 Contact a Family, 2009: Our family, our future, London: Contact a Family

2 Contact a Family, 2009: Our family, our future, London: Contact a Family: 62

3 Contact a Family, 2009a: What makes my family stronger: a report into what makes families with disabled children stronger – socially, emotionally and practically, London: Contact a Family

4 Contact a Family, 2009a: What makes my family stronger: a report into what makes families with disabled children stronger – socially, emotionally and practically, London: Contact a Family

5 Gray DE, 1993: Perceptions of Stigma: the Parents of Autistic Children, in Sociology of Health and Illness, 15 (1) 102–120:110

6 Ryan S, 2004: 'Busy Behaviour' in the 'Land of the Golden M': going out with learning disabled children in public places, in Journal of Applied Research in Intellectual Disabilities (18) 65–74

7 Ablon J, 2002: The Nature of Stigma and Medical Conditions, in Epilepsy and Behaviour, 3 (6S2) 2–9

8 Sayce L, 1998: Stigma, Discrimination and Social Exclusion: what's in a word?, in Journal of Mental Health (7) 331–343

Noah and that he would have to leave.'[9]

In the same vein, a recent survey by the National Autistic Society investigated public perceptions of autism. One respondent stated that:

'My family have been threatened to be evicted from our house as our neighbours have complained about my child head-banging on the walls. The Authority won't help us to make adaptations to the house to have soft-padded walls.'[10]

The consequences of stigma

A number of different facets of the experience of being stigmatised as a parent are exemplified in this quote from the mother of a girl with autism:

'I'm not a human being. I'm only the mother of a handicapped daughter and I don't have a mind of my own. You often get that. Oh, people that know me probably wouldn't although they might think it, you know, but generally you get treated as if you're an imbecile too… and you think "Oh, that's just me […] I'm not a normal person […]". They tend to forget that you're still a normal person like them and you want to lead a normal life.'[11] We can detect here:

⇨ The sense of being made to feel different to one's peers: I'm not a human being […] I'm not a normal person.

⇨ Self-denigration, thus internalising the stigma: I'm only the mother of a handicapped daughter and I don't have a mind of my own.

⇨ Imputing negative attitudes to others, even friends: you often get that. Oh, people that know me probably wouldn't although they might think it, you know.

⇨ Stigmatisation by association: generally you get treated as if you're an imbecile too.

⇨ Defensive adherence to an eroding sense of self: they tend to forget that you're still a normal

person like them and you want to lead a normal life.

Courtesy stigma and the parents of children with disabilities

Researchers generally agree that the parents of children with disabilities experience what Goffman[12] defined as 'courtesy stigma'. Courtesy stigma is a stigma of affiliation, which can attach to an individual as a consequence of their association with stigmatised groups, rather than as a result of any innate attribute or behaviour. In the context of families of a child with disabilities, parents may become the object of courtesy stigma simply because of their relationship with the child and not because of any shared disability.

The stigma experienced by parents of children with disabilities

This article examines the stigma experienced by parents of children with disabilities. For the purposes of this article, 'child with disabilities' refers to children with a neurological condition, such as cerebral palsy, autistic spectrum disorder, epilepsy, learning disabilities, attention deficit hyperactivity disorder, behaviour and emotional problems, and developmental delay. The effects of such stigma should not be underestimated, not least because it is experienced in addition to, and alongside the range of challenges and stressors which the arrival of a child with disabilities in a family brings. Beresford observes that 'most parents found the stresses associated with the care of their disabled child to be wide-ranging, unrelenting and sometimes overwhelming'.[13] Researchers distinguish between 'enacted' stigma and 'felt' stigma.[14] Felt stigma refers to parents' internalised feelings of shame and the fear of being rejected or excluded

by others. Enacted stigma refers to instances of outright discrimination or exclusion experienced by parents.

The experience of felt stigma

Investigating the experience of felt and enacted stigma by parents of children with high functioning autism, Gray[15] found that slightly more than 75% of parents had experienced felt stigma: 'Most commonly parents imagined that others were critical of their child-raising abilities, not accepting of them and made them feel embarrassed.'[16] Embarrassment was the most common form of felt stigma which parents reported, most often experienced in the everyday social settings in which parents find themselves with their children. As one of Gray's respondents relates: 'We went on a… camp and we were pretty apprehensive about going … We were the only ones with an autistic child and … he performed in front of all those people there and had to take charge. And he called me an idiot in front of all those people, and swearing started to come out, and everybody just freezes. Everybody is just embarrassed.'[17]

This experience of felt stigma is echoed by the parent of a young woman with Asperger syndrome:

'People don't understand her behaviour – why she's so antisocial on some occasions and why on others, she is so effusive. She tries to mimic social behaviour, but it's exaggerated. She can go from being quite nasty with some people to being obsequious with others, almost fawning. People don't know how to cope with that sort of behaviour.'[18]

The experience of enacted stigma: avoidance

Conversely, only about half of Gray's respondents had experienced enacted stigma, which generally took three main forms: avoidance, overtly

9 Contact a Family, 2009: Our family, our future, London: Contact a Family: 17

10 National Autistic Society, 2007: Think differently

11 Gray DE, 1993: Perceptions of Stigma: the Parents of Autistic Children, in Sociology of Health and Illness, 15 (1) 102–120:109

12 Goffman E, 1963: Stigma: Notes on the Management of Spoiled Identity, Englewood Cliffs, NJ: Prentice-Hall

13 Beresford B, 1994: Caring for a Severely Disabled Child, Social Care Research 54, Joseph Rowntree Foundation: 1

14 Scambler G and Hopkins A, 1986: Being Epileptic: Coming to Terms with Stigma, in Sociology of Health and Illness 8 (1) 26–43

15 Gray DE, 2002: 'Everybody just freezes. Everybody is just embarrassed': felt and enated stigma among parents of children with high functioning autism, in Sociology of Health and Illness 24 (6) 734–749

16 Ibid.: 739

17 Ibid.: 740

18 National Autistic Society, 2007: Think differently – act positively: public perceptions of autism, London: National Autistic Society: 15

hostile staring, and rude comments. Of these, the most common was avoidance. Other research has also revealed that social exclusion is widely experienced by the parents of children with disabilities, even to the point of immediate and extended family staying away. In Mencap's 2001 survey, many parents responded to this effect, as the two quotes below exemplify:

'Neither grandparents offered to take Bradley for a walk. My mum used to babysit once in a blue moon, as long as he was in bed. I think it's because they did not accept Bradley as a person in his own right.'

'My brother was never interested. My mother never bathed her, fed her or babysat for her. They just stayed away because of all sorts of excuses. They never tried.'[19]

Avoidance can also be more subtly expressed:

'… they never ask about the child at all, never. And then they'll be talking about something and you might say to them "How's your child getting on?" or something and they'd say "fine" and then that's it.'[20]

The experience of enacted stigma: hostile staring

The second form of enacted stigma, overtly hostile staring, is also typically experienced by parents in everyday settings where they, and other families, habitually go with their children. Saskia is ten years old and has multiple disabilities. Her mother writes that:

'It is difficult taking Saskia out on my own and can be soul-destroying. There are very few places that I can take Saskia before we are stared at and asked to leave. I now have to warn people before I go.'[21]

Speech bubbles: "OH DEAR – ASPERGER'S!!" / "TEXT BOOK AVOIDANCE…"

Similarly, the following is a quote from the mother of an eight-year-old boy with autism:

'I usually get stares and tuts from people who just think I'm a bad mother. I even once had a woman in a supermarket tell me that I shouldn't take my son out in public even after I explained that he is autistic.'[22]

The experience of enacted stigma: rude comments

The third form of enacted stigma, making rude comments, is experienced by many parents of children with disabilities. As the National Autistic Society reports:

'In shops, in restaurants, on public transport – every day and in all sorts of places, parents face lack of understanding and intolerance and this in turn causes considerable stress and anxiety.'[23]

One of the respondents in the National Autistic Society's survey, the parent of a six-year-old boy with autism, stated:

'He didn't used to like going into supermarkets […]. He would scream as soon as he went in. People would come up and say to me, "if that was my child, I'd smack him" or "he needs a good slap". People

pass so many comments you've got to grow a thick skin otherwise you'd stay in all the time.'[24]

For parents, it may be difficult to ignore this kind of unwarranted attention. The parent of Davis, a young boy with autism, relates the following:

'The unfamiliar surroundings were making Davis anxious and he was whining. "Give him a slap," growled the young workman. There was an awkward silence from the other people in the café. "He has a disability," I said. The workman retreated into his paper. The others relaxed and returned to what they were doing. It had worked.'[25]

Accounting for variation in the degree of courtesy stigma experienced: mother or father?

Researchers tend to agree that, as it is the mother who is far more likely to be the parent who takes the child with a disability out into the world, she deals far more with public encounters and hence, with the experience of courtesy stigma that these encounters can entail. Indeed, Gray[26] found that mothers of children with disabilities are

19 Mencap, 2001: No ordinary life: the support needs of families caring for children and adults with profound and multiple learning disabilities, London: Mencap: 13

20 Gray DE, 1993: Perceptions of Stigma: the Parents of Autistic Children, in Sociology of Health and Illness, 15 (1) 102–120:109

21 Contact a Family, 2009: Our family, our future, London: Contact a Family: 21

22 National Autistic Society, 2007: Think differently – act positively: public perceptions of autism, London: National Autistic Society: 11

23 Ibid.: 15

24 Ibid.: 10

25 Ibid.: 15

26 Gray DE, 2002: 'Everybody just freezes. Everybody is just embarrassed': felt and enacted stigma among parents of children with high functioning autism, in Sociology of Health and Illness 24 (6) 734–749

much more likely than fathers to experience stigma, both felt and enacted. Another possible explanation is that mothers can often feel considerable guilt for their child's disability[27] and are likely to feel more responsible for the successful presentation of the family in the public realm, whether they are full-time mothers or have employment outside the home. For a mother who experiences especially high levels of felt stigma, a consequence may be that her child interacts less frequently with their age peers at home or in the community.[28]

Accounting for variation in the degree of courtesy stigma experienced: visibility of the child's disability

A second variable which can influence the degree of courtesy stigma experienced by the parent of a child with disabilities is the visibility or otherwise of the child's disability – the more apparent the disability, the fewer stigmatising reactions are experienced, and the less outwardly apparent the disability, the greater the experience of stigma. This is because, in the case of a child with little or no outward sign of disability, members of the public are unable to find an explanation for any 'socially unacceptable behaviour' that the child might produce, other than by blaming it on bad behaviour, poor parenting or a mixture of the two.

Accounting for variation in the degree of courtesy stigma experienced: severity of the child's symptoms

The degree of courtesy stigma experienced by the parent of a child with disabilities can also be influenced by the severity of the behavioural symptoms which

the child exhibits, with parents of children who can be aggressive or violent being far more likely to experience enacted stigma than parents of children who may be less disruptive. The reasons for this are, simply, that a child who is more aggressive is more likely to disturb those around them and hence, more likely to provoke a strong reaction. The social challenges this must present to the child's parents are not difficult to imagine.

Conclusion

This article has shown how public perceptions of disability can exert a negative influence on the lives of parents of a child with disabilities, adding appreciably to the already considerable challenges they face in caring for their child, and in negotiating public encounters. This negative influence is experienced in the form of courtesy stigma, whereby the stigma which attaches to the child because of their disability, is extended to the parents, simply as a function of their relationship with their child.

The courtesy stigma experienced by the parents of a child with disabilities remains little researched and incompletely understood. In particular, very little long-term research has been undertaken to investigate the experience of courtesy stigma over time, interviewing the parents and then, after a period of years, interviewing them again to chart any changes or developments

in their experience of stigma. The little research of this nature that has been carried out, suggests that, whilst parents do continue to experience courtesy stigma, after the passage of time it begins to matter less to them, and becomes less threatening to their self-esteem. There is, therefore, a need to design and carry out long-term research investigating the experience of courtesy stigma by parents of children with disabilities. Such a study could begin to shed light on an aspect of parenting a child with disabilities that, to date, has received too little attention, given the extent to which parents perceive and experience such stigma as an additional burden in already stretched lives.

This information is not meant to replace the advice of any physician or qualified health professional. The information provided by Cerebra is for information purposes only and is not a substitute for medical advice or treatment for any medical condition. You should promptly seek professional medical assistance if you have concerns regarding any health issue.

First published 2011.

10 June 2013

27 Anderson JM and Elfert H, 1989: Managing Chronic Illness in the Family: women as caretakers, in Journal of Advanced Nursing (14) 735–743

28 Green SE, 2003: 'What do you mean, 'what's wrong with her?'': stigma and the lives of families and children with disabilities, in Social Science and Medicine (57) 1361–1374

Disability rights

Overview

As a disabled person, you have rights to protect you from discrimination. These rights cover most areas including:

⇨ employment

⇨ education

⇨ dealing with the police.

The Equality Act 2010 and the United Nations (UN) Convention on disability rights help to enforce, protect and promote your rights.

Employment

It's against the law for employers to discriminate against you because of a disability. The Equality Act 2010 protects you and covers areas including:

⇨ application forms

⇨ interview arrangements

⇨ aptitude or proficiency tests

⇨ job offers

⇨ terms of employment, including pay

⇨ promotion, transfer and training opportunities

⇨ dismissal or redundancy

⇨ discipline and grievances.

Reasonable adjustments in the workplace

An employer has to make 'reasonable adjustments' to avoid you being put at a disadvantage compared to non-disabled people in the workplace. For example, adjusting your working hours or providing you with a special piece of equipment to help you do the job.

Recruitment

An employer who's recruiting staff may make limited enquiries about your health or disability.

You can only be asked about your health or disability:

⇨ to help decide if you can carry out a task that is an essential part of the work

⇨ to help find out if you can take part in an interview

⇨ to help decide if the interviewers need to make reasonable adjustments for you in a selection process

⇨ to help monitoring

⇨ if they want to increase the number of disabled people they employ

⇨ if they need to know for the purposes of national security checks.

You may be asked whether you have a health condition or disability on an application form or in an interview. You need to think about whether the question is one that is allowed to be asked at that stage of recruitment.

Redundancy and retirement

You can't be chosen for redundancy just because you're disabled. The selection process for redundancy must be fair and balanced for all employees.

Your employer cannot force you to retire if you become disabled.

Education

It's against the law for a school or other education provider to treat disabled students unfavourably. This includes:

⇨ 'direct discrimination' – e.g. refusing admission to a student because of disability

⇨ 'indirect discrimination' – e.g. only providing application forms in one format that may not be accessible

⇨ 'discrimination arising from a disability' – e.g. a disabled pupil is prevented from going outside at break time because it takes too long to get there

⇨ 'harassment' – e.g. a teacher shouts at a disabled student for not paying attention when the student's disability stops them from easily concentrating

⇨ victimisation – e.g. suspending a disabled student because they've complained about harassment.

Reasonable adjustments

An education provider has a duty to make 'reasonable adjustments' to make sure disabled students are not discriminated against. These changes could include:

- ⇨ changes to physical features – e.g. creating a ramp so that students can enter a classroom
- ⇨ providing extra support and aids (such as specialist teachers or equipment).

Special Educational Needs (SEN)

All publicly-funded pre-schools, nurseries, state schools and local authorities must try to identify and help assess children with Special Educational Needs.

If a child has a statement of special educational needs, they should have a 'transition plan' drawn up in Year 9. This helps to plan what support the child will have after leaving school.

Higher education

All universities and higher education colleges should have a person in charge of disability issues that you can talk to about the support they offer.

You can also ask local social services for an assessment to help with your day-to-day living needs.

Police

If you're being questioned or interviewed at a police station, you've certain rights depending on your impairment.

Deaf, hearing-impaired or speech difficulties

The police should arrange for an interpreter to be present with you. The police can interview you without an interpreter if a delay would result in harm to people, property or evidence.

Learning disabilities

The police should only interview someone who has a learning disability when a responsible person (referred to as an 'appropriate adult') is present. The appropriate adult should not work for the police and should have

experience of people with learning disabilities. The police can interview you without an appropriate adult if a delay would result in harm to people, property or evidence.

Right to medical treatment

If you're being kept in a police cell, you've the right to a medical examination by a healthcare worker. A healthcare worker may be a paramedic, nurse or a police surgeon (sometimes referred to as a 'Forensic Medical Examiner').

If you do not want to be examined by the healthcare worker provided, you could be examined by a general practitioner (GP) that you choose – if they're available. You may have to pay for this, and this payment will be noted down.

The Equality Act 2010 and UN Convention

The Equality Act 2010 protects you from discrimination. It provides legal rights for you in the areas of:

- ⇨ employment
- ⇨ education
- ⇨ access to goods, services and facilities
- ⇨ buying and renting land or property.

The Equality Act 2010 also protects your rights if you have an association with a disabled person, e.g. a carer or parent.

Get more information about the Equality Act 2010 from the Government Equalities Office.

United Nations (UN) Convention on disability rights

The UN Convention on disability rights has been agreed by the UK to protect and promote the rights of disabled people.

Get more information about the UN Convention on disability rights from the Office for Disability Issues.

Further help and advice

You can get further advice and information on your rights from:

- ⇨ Equality Advisory Support Service
- ⇨ Disability Rights UK
- ⇨ Advicenow
- ⇨ Citizens Advice.

30 May 2013

- ⇨ The above information is reprinted with kind permission from Cerebra. Please visit www.cerebra.org.uk for further information.

Work Choice – is it working?

The Government's employment support programmes for disabled people are facing scrutiny, following the publication of a report conducted by Disability Rights UK.

By Petra Acred

When they came into office three years ago, the Coalition Government faced a difficult challenge: how to improve the prospects of getting disabled people into work when the last Government's *Pathways to Work* programme was a failure. Their solution was to introduce Work Choice (a replacement for WORKSTEP and Work Preparation) and Work Programme, both with the aims of supporting disabled people who are seeking work. These are centralised employment programmes on a large scale, but, three years into the Coalition's term, just how effective have they been?

Work Choice was established to help disabled people who faced the most barriers to securing employment. It promised a more personalised approach, tailored to the individual's needs, through training, confidence building and interview coaching. It has been criticised in the report by Disability Rights UK, however, as failing the very people it was set up to help. Since 2011/2012, Work Choice has helped only 58 people with serious mental health problems to find work and, in general, it has been found not to be serving those with the most complex needs who are most in need of help. It is suggested that this is due to the 'outcome payment model', which sees incentives given for proven results; it may be easier, therefore, to work with individuals with the fewest barriers to their employment. This would provide a service that is driven by financial reward and impressive statistics as opposed to helping those who are most in need of support and encouragement.

Disregarding the fact that Work Choice appears to be ignoring those most in need, it has still only helped 31% of those on the programme to secure employment; a failure on both levels.

The Work Programme, which provides up to two years of work experience and training for disabled people, has had even less success. Figures from July 2013 have shown that only 5.3% of new Employment and Support Allowance claimants had secured employment through the Work Programme. This incredibly low statistic is one that falls beneath even the Government's modest aims of 16.5% of people claiming disability benefit securing employment through the programme.

So where is it all going wrong? Findings suggest that the support on offer is not reaching those who need it and that, when it does, it is often ineffective. Most respondents to the research conducted by Disability Rights UK had not been supported by the Work Programme, suggesting that it might not be widely available or that it is not seen as a valuable source of support. Conversely, respondents said that the majority of support they received came from other sources such as family, friends or disability organisations – not Government programmes. Having said that, 63% of people surveyed felt that the support they received from any combination of sources had not helped them to get a job.

The fact that the majority of respondents were not supported by the Work Programme may be due to a lack of awareness; 78% said that they would like to know more about the types of support on offer and the resources available to them. 58% of the respondents to the survey said that they would like a personalised plan; something only 36% of them already had in place despite the findings of research that have shown a personalised approach to be more successful long-term.

So what is the solution? A major issue is the mishandling of money: the Work Programme is projected to cost £3–5 billion over a five-year period and it is simply not working. The general, centralised approaches, too, are failing and there is a continued lack of consistent and inclusive opportunities for those with disabilities.

The report by Disability Rights UK suggests that that more work experience and training is vital in getting disabled people into the workplace and that the best way of doing this is to cut out 'the middleman' that controls and transfers money. This would see control given directly to disabled people and employers instead of the incentivised providers of the programmes. The report found that disabled people are desperate for a voice; to be consulted on the form their support takes and how money to help them is spent. Combined with employers who want to positively change the lives of people with the enthusiasm, potential and desire to learn and succeed, a drastic change that involves the very people the programmes affect seems to be an essential overhaul.

The failure of the current programmes, emphasises the barriers that disabled people continue to face when seeking employment. Everyone has the right to work and the right to be given appropriate support and advice when they face challenges in doing so. The Government's failings, particularly the apparent discrimination within the Work Choice programme and its continued lack of success, have highlighted the desperate need for change.

Source:

http://www.disabilityrightsuk.org/sites/default/files/pdf/

Taking Control of Employment Support, Disability Rights UK, October 2013

1 November 2013

© *Petra Acred/Independence Educational Publishers 2013*

Disability confident

The Government launches an advertising campaign to help businesses become more confident about recruiting disabled people.

A two-year advertising campaign to support businesses to become more confident at recruiting disabled people is being launched by the Government at the UK's first national Disability Employment Conference.

It comes as new research published this week shows that more disabled jobseekers cite employers' attitudes (42%) as a barrier to work than transport difficulties (37%).

Around 300 employers, including FTSE 100 companies, small businesses and disabled entrepreneurs will be in attendance at the conference – the first Government conference of its kind – to improve employment outcomes for disabled people.

Plans for a new service for employers specifically for helping disabled people into work – and which make it easier for businesses to hire and keep disabled people in work – will also be on the agenda.

The conference will bring together employers who are exemplars in areas of best practice in disability employment, others who want to improve the diversity of their workforce and where disabled people are under-represented as employees.

There are 6.9 million disabled people of working age in Great Britain, and the employment rate for disabled people has increased gradually over the years from 42.2% in 2002 to 46.3% in 2012.

Prime Minister David Cameron said:

'I am delighted we are holding this first Disability Employment Conference and launching this new campaign to help employers become confident employing disabled people. This isn't just about doing what is right for disabled people. Employing disabled people makes business sense too.

'We need to break the myth about the complexities of employing disabled people, or to put it more simply – to give employers confidence. That is why we are launching this Disability Confident campaign.'

Minister for Disabled People Esther McVey said:

'Last year's Paralympics truly captivated the hearts of the nation and have undoubtedly helped shift attitudes and perceptions towards disabled people.

'And although the employment rates for disabled people have increased gradually over the years, there's more we need to do as too often the talents of disabled people in the workforce are left untapped.

'That is why we are hosting the UK's first national Disability Employment Conference to see how we can harness the drive and innovation of the private sector. It will start a campaign by employers, for employers to better recognise the considerable talents disabled people have to offer and challenge some of the preconceptions around employing disabled people.

'We've already helped boost employment opportunities for disabled people through our schemes and we are committed to doing everything possible to help disabled people into mainstream work.'

To help support employers overcome barriers and become disability confident, from today the Government will:

⇨ host a series of regional Business Breakfasts on proposals for a dedicated employer service, focusing on business needs – funded from the £350 million budget for support for people with disabilities and health conditions

⇨ roll out a new £500,000 two-year Government campaign targeting employers' and workforce attitudes to hiring disabled people

⇨ support the roll out of business-led commitments to hire more disabled people

⇨ support disabled people and media organisations increase media representation and portrayal of disabled people in mainstream programmes

⇨ provide opportunities, through changes announced this week to Access to Work, for employers to engage disabled people on work experience, traineeship and supported internships

⇨ provide streamlined advice and support for employers on hiring and keeping disabled people in work through our guidance on employing disabled people and people with health conditions.

The new service for employers will focus on supporting them to become more confident about hiring disabled people.

The conference at the QEII Conference Centre in Westminster today (18 July 2013), will include keynote speeches from Secretary of State Iain Duncan Smith, Business Secretary Vince Cable, CEO of Barclays Retail and Business Banking Ashok Vaswani, and Sir Andrew Witty CEO of GSK.

If you want to follow the Disability Employment Conference – join in the conversation with #DisabilityConfident on Twitter.

More information

Research shows that 42% of disabled people looking for work say employers' attitudes are a barrier to work, compared with 37% who say that transport is.

If disabled people's employment rate matched that of the rest of the population, an extra two million disabled people would be working.

The 'disability pound' is worth £80 billion to the GB economy, and one in five customers is likely to be disabled.

More than 25,000 disabled people have moved into jobs, training or work placements through the Government's package of employment support over the past two years – Get Britain Working measures – since they were introduced in 2011.

The Government's specialist disability employment scheme, Access to Work, helps more than 30,000 disabled employees and entrepreneurs get or stay in work each year. Research shows that around half (45%) of Access to Work customers would be out of work if they did not receive support through the scheme.

The Minister for Disabled People has also said that DWP will work with its providers so that the £3.5 billion 'buying power' can be utilised to increase employment opportunities for disabled people.

Remploy Employment Services also found 50,000 jobs for disabled and disadvantaged people since 2010 – many with similar disabilities to those working in Remploy factories.

Access to Work has previously been called 'the Government's best kept secret', so to raise awareness of the changes, the Government has expanded the marketing campaign to target particularly young disabled people and people with mental health conditions.

Disabled people can get support through Access to Work when setting up their own business if they are enrolled on the New Enterprise Allowance. The New Enterprise Allowance provides expert coaching and financial support for jobseekers with a business idea.

Employer story

Dave Hawkins is the Managing Director of Cyclone Technologies. A leading supplier of bespoke, lightweight wheelchairs, they are the UK's foremost rehabilitation and training specialist.

Dave, who himself is paraplegic, says he prides himself on his workforce. With an expert team boasting 120 years' combined experience of life in a wheelchair, their main objective is to transform the lives of disabled people by helping them regain a new level of independence and control in their lives.

Dave says...

'I think when an employer is looking for a good accountant; they should find a good accountant. And if that accountant happens to be a wheelchair user or has an arm missing or a speech impediment, if he is a good accountant then why will it matter?'

Employee story

Chris Chegwen is a mobility specialist at Cyclone Technologies. He had an accident as a teenager and has been in a wheelchair for over 30 years.

He says he was lucky because shortly after his accident he asked a local employer for a job in his accounts office.

Chris was 19 years old and thinks he was lucky that he was taken on straight away. At the time he was studying accountancy at the local college but he climbed through the ranks of the company and eventually became a part-owner!

Chris says...

'These days there are lots of ways your workplace can be adjusted or even physically altered to make it accessible. You've still got your brain, so go out there and use it!'

18 July 2013

⇨ The above information is reprinted with kind permission from GOV.UK. Please visit www.gov.uk for further information.

© Crown copyright 2013

Disabled people 'hit by multiple benefit cuts'

Hundreds of thousands of disabled people will be worse off as a result of six different benefit cuts, according to Scope.

The charity says the Government's welfare reforms will lead to up to 3.7 million disabled people losing a total of £28.3 billion by 2018.

A study carried out by the think tank Demos for Scope looks at cuts to disability living allowance (DLA), employment and support allowance (ESA), housing benefit and the so-called 'bedroom tax'.

It reaches the conclusion that the changes, which come into effect in April, will hit 'the same group of disabled people over and over again'.

Scope Chief Executive Richard Hawkes told Channel 4 News: 'It's a bleak picture. It seems incredible that just a little over six months ago we were talking about the Paralympics having changed the way we see disability. What's happened?

'The Paralympics were a breakthrough moment. Disability had never been so visible, so talked about.

'At the moment it's not the done thing to say the state needs to spend money. But if we want to live in a country where disabled people can pay the bills, can live independently in the community, where they can work, have relationships and ultimately be visible then that's exactly what needs to happen.'

'Triple whammy'

The research suggests that 26,000 people face a 'triple whammy' of having their ESA capped at one per cent before losing their ESA and DLA – costing them up to £4,600 a year.

'It's a bleak picture. It seems incredible that just a little over six months ago we were talking about the Paralympics having changed the way we see disability. What's happened?'

It says 3,000 people will be hit by six different cuts, losing £23,300 by 2018.

Demos Deputy Director Claudia Wood, lead researcher on the project, said disabled people were 'bearing the brunt' of the Government's welfare cuts.

She added: 'What's shocking is that the Government doesn't assess the likely combined impact of these changes, only the impact of each change individually.

'However, many disabled families are being affected by combinations of four, five and even six changes...'

'Scaremongering'

A DWP spokesperson said: 'There's a lot of misleading stories about the impact of our welfare reforms on disabled people, which could lead to unnecessary scaremongering.

'Our reforms will make sure the billions we spend every year give more targeted support and better reflect today's understanding of disability.

'Hundreds of thousands of disabled adults and children will actually receive more support than now with the combined effect of benefit changes under universal credit.'

18 July 2013

⇨ The above information is reprinted with kind permission from Channel 4 News. Please visit www.channel4.com/news for further information.

Victory for disability campaigners over Independent Living Fund

The Government's decision to scrap a scheme designed to help disabled people to live independently did not properly consider the 'potentially very grave impact' on the lives of vulnerable people, the Court of Appeal has ruled.

The fight against the abolition of the Independent Living Fund was taken to the courts by five disabled people, arguing that 20,000 severely disabled people have had their lives shattered by the removal of the fund, and that their views had not been fully taken into account.

Gabriel Pepper, from Walthamstow, east London was one of them. He accused the Government of imposing 'appalling cuts' which were 'a vicious attack on the disabled'. The other applicants are Stuart Bracking, Paris L'amour, Anne Pridmore and John Aspinall, who brought his case with his mother, Evonne Taylforth, acting as his litigation friend.

But the impact of the ruling goes beyond the five. Waiting outside the Royal Courts of Justice in the rain, sat in her wheelchair, supporter Jenny Hurst said she had been 'sick with worry' but she was delighted.

'It is a huge relief to have got over this first hurdle. There is more to go but we have got over this first hurdle, which is fantastic,' she said.

Welcoming the 'powerful' ruling, law firms Deighton Pierce-Glynn and Scott-Moncrieff & Associates, which represented the claimants, said their clients had 'feared that the loss of their ILF support would threaten their right to live with dignity, and that they could be forced into residential care or lose their ability to work and participate in everyday activities on an equal footing with other people'.

'It remains to be seen whether the Government will seek to revisit the idea of closing the fund. However, it confirmed in the course of the proceedings that any preparatory steps were at an early stage and could be reversed if necessary.

'Any fresh decision would require the Government to go back to the drawing board and to take into account the wealth of concerns raised by disabled people and by local authorities about the proposal to close the fund.

'Any new decision must be taken with proper attention to the Government's legal obligations to take account of the impact on disabled people and to consider alternatives that would avoid that impact.'

The appeal by the five was against a High Court ruling by Mr Justice Blake in April that the closure decision was lawful.

The five argued that the High Court had gone wrong in law and there was a lack of proper consultation before the closure decision was taken on 18 December 2012.

Appeal judges Lord Justice Elias, Lord Justice Kitchin and Lord Justice McCombe allowed the challenge and quashed the 18 December decision.

In the case of the five there was 'simply not the evidence' to demonstrate to the court 'that a focused regard was had to the potentially very grave impact upon individuals in this group of disabled persons, within the context of a consideration of the statutory requirements for disabled people as a whole', said Lord Justice McCombe.

He continued: 'It seems to me that what was put before the minister did not give to her an adequate flavour of the responses received indicating that independent living might well be put seriously in peril for a large number of people.'

Lord Justice Elias agreed, saying: 'Any government, particularly in a time of austerity, is obliged to take invidious decisions which may exceptionally bear harshly on some of the most disadvantaged in society.'

The court did not seek to 'curb government's powers to take such decisions, but it does require government to confront the anticipated consequences in a conscientious and deliberate way insofar as they impact upon the equality objectives.'

6 November 2013

⇨ The above information is reprinted with kind permission from *The Huffington Post UK*. Please visit www.huffingtonpost.co.uk for further information.

New research shows significant economic benefits from providing social care to disabled people

The National Autistic Society, alongside Mencap, Scope, Sense and Leonard Cheshire Disability, has published a new report showing that investing in social care prevents disabled people falling into crisis, and as a result, leads to substantial economic benefits.

The in-depth study sets out that every £1 spent on services generates benefits to people, carers, local and central Government worth an average of £1.30.

The study comes as the social care crisis debate about who gets care and how it's funded continues to make the headlines and as the Government's Care Bill continues to make its way through Parliament.

The experts at Deloitte who worked with the charities on the report, analysed four services, including The National Autistic Society's Horizons service, that are all used by disabled people who need a lower level of care – which may be just a few hours a week and could help with budgeting or timekeeping, for example.

The research showed that these services can prevent people's needs escalating and can prevent people from having to rely on more costly care and support. These types of service can also promote quality of life and engagement with society as well as reduce dependency on family members and carers.

The five charities warn that if the Government sets the bar on who receives care too high, we will not realise the potential financial and personal benefits from these types of services.

Mark Lever, Chief Executive of the National Autistic Society, said:

⇨ The financial case is crystal clear: the Government must act now to address the inherent flaws in the social care system and ensure people with autism and other disabilities receive the support they desperately need.

⇨ Currently, many people with autism miss out on this support as their difficulties aren't recognised; in most cases eligibility criteria are set too high and assessors lack the training in the disability they need, to understand its daily impact.

⇨ As a result many people with autism can eventually plunge into crisis, meaning they require very expensive and intensive support. This could be easily averted if simple and relatively low-cost options are put in place in the first instance, such as befriending services or social skills training. This would not only benefit the public purse but also have a tremendous human impact, transforming the lives of thousands of people for the better.'

Read the full report *Ending the Other Care Crisis: Making the case for investment in preventative care and support for disabled adults* at www.autism.org.uk.

18 July 2013

⇨ The above information is reprinted with kind permission from The National Autistic Society. Please visit www.autism.org.uk for further information.

Have you been on the end of scrounger abuse?

It's now almost a year since the Paralympics started and we've been asking disabled people and their families if they feel the games made a difference to their day-to-day lives.

There'll be a lot of discussion next week about legacy. Scope is going to be urging journalists and the Government to listen to disabled people's views.

One issue that keeps coming up is 'benefits scrounger rhetoric', and how this leads to people being abused in the street and being trolled online.

We asked on Twitter and Facebook for people to share their own experiences.

Bullying and abuse

Some people responded with shocking stories of unprovoked verbal and physical abuse:

'Just the other night one Twitter account dedicated to highlighting the abuse of blue badge bays decided to shut down because of the abuse it gets. One of my friends is seeking a judicial review and they tried to use his Twitter use against him. I have a specific troll who tells me I am just lazy, I could work if I tried and so-on. Any time there is a documentary-style TV programme featuring sick or disabled people it stirs up a lot of abuse and general ignorance.' *Ema via email*

'I'm leaning on my crutches by the broccoli when a lady in her late-50s walks up behind me, shoves me hard into the broccoli box – face first – and calls me a disability scrounging unrepeatable in front of my children. My most embarrassing moment.' *Tinna on Facebook*

'Someone walked into the back of my wheelchair whilst in a supermarket queue, which apparently is my fault as "your sort shouldn't be cluttering up the shops".' *Teddy on Facebook*

And it's not just from strangers:

'I've had 'friends' explain how I just have to accept and expect romantic rejection because disability is ugly.' *NQ videos on Twitter*

'I was told by a 'friend' that I shouldn't be allowed a mobility car for my wheelchair-using son with CP.'[1] *Naomi on Twitter*

Hidden disability

Many people spoke about the problem of impairments that aren't immediately obvious:

'I was once accused of stealing a disabled persons' bus pass. It had my name and my photo on. I am partially sighted. You can't see the damage I have to my optic nerves, nor how much I can really see... I've had someone tell me I shouldn't be on Disability Living Allowance (DLA) because there's nothing wrong with me. I don't feel the need to broadcast every single medical problem I have.' *Sofie on Facebook*

'People seem to think that 'disability' means a missing leg, or using a wheelchair/crutches; it can be, but sometimes a disability affects people more subtly and they still need assistance.' *Caitlin on Facebook*

'I have epilepsy and hold a bus pass because of it – I've had some dirty looks off people for using it in the past.' *Kath on Facebook*

Unashamed and fighting back

Some disabled people told us that they refuse to be ashamed of the money they receive and are fighting back at the bullies:

'I'm not ashamed of having claimed out of work benefits and I refuse to be ashamed of my DLA.' *Natalya on Facebook*

'If anyone abuses me they get far worse back. I am sick and tired of being abused because of something that is no fault of my own. I will not be bullied or abused by people who believe the rhetoric.' *Ian on Facebook*

Parents told us that they didn't care what people thought – the well-being of their children comes first:

'I have a two-year-old with CP. There would be no way I could take him to his physio without the extra help we get through DLA. If that makes me a beggar then so be it. I really don't care as long as my son gets the best possible care and start in life!' *Darren on Facebook*

'My daughter has CP. I listen to people going on about benefits and get fed up with listening to the constant moaning. I only want what is best for her and for those that do complain about disabled – stop and think – how would they feel if it was them?' *Val on Facebook*

Whilst some parents are taking more extreme measures!

'My son has severe CP. Rules we are working on when he is in his electric chair are:

⇨ If someone stares: smile at them. If they still stare: run them over.

⇨ Three 'excuse me's' from Mum and Dad and if they still won't shift: run them over.

⇨ Three honks on his horn then... yup: run them over.' *Wag on Facebook*

⇨ The above information is reprinted with kind permission from Scope. Please visit www.scope.org.uk for further information.

1 Cerebral palsy

© Scope 2013

Why I'm lobbying Parliament for disabled rights

The right to live freely and with dignity should be available to all, yet the Government threatens our most basic, hard-won rights.

By Penny Pepper

I arrived earlier this week to deliver a poetry workshop. I discovered that there was no obvious wheelchair access to the building as refurbishments were taking place. A bold arrow points to a door declaring alternative access. There are two large concrete steps – which amounts to a no-entry sign for me as a wheelchair user.

This tiny, familiar incident is not directly connected to why I'm going to lobby Parliament on Wednesday to demand equality and inclusion, but it is indicative of my world where many barriers remain. And they are increasing; seasoned with the sour taste of growing numbers of hate crimes and the fallout of pervasive scapegoating of disabled citizens. Yet I believe that worst of all are the Government's policies and an ideology that seems to have singled out us disabled people to carry a very heavy and disproportionate austerity burden. The hard-won paltry rights for which we have given blood and sweat, stand in fear of regression, if not a complete dismantling. Let me speak plainly: we are not losing privileges, we are losing essentials.

And so I fight with my colleagues from Disabled People Against the Cuts (DPAC) and Wednesday is the day of the Freedom Drive rally to demand equality and inclusion for disabled people. I act with deeds and words, because the Government seems determined to resurrect the old Victorian approach to disabled people. We must be grateful; we must accept cuts; we must accept charity; we must be cap in hand.

The personal is political; and for me this is made explicit with the Government's decision to close down the independent living fund (ILF) in 2015. This fund tops up local authority money to enable those individuals, like myself, deemed

'severely disabled', to hire staff or services in order to live full lives, independently at home. The word 'live' is key – opposed to existing. I work with the skills I have; the reality that I need assistance to get out of bed in the morning is neither here nor there when it comes to me, the writer. But of course, it is crucial to my daily life, and I believe that this simple right to live freely with dignity should be available to everyone based on need.

And so I campaign and I lobby. Last week at an ILF event I released a balloon, a metaphor for freedom. On this I wrote a message for Iain Duncan Smith: 'YOU sleep in YOUR s***' Not subtle, but that is the reality many of us face.

Simultaneously to that action, I was asked to comment on research which shows that the hopes for a marvellous lasting legacy, post-Paralympic Games, for your ordinary disabled citizen, has not materialised. I don't enjoy being smug; I expressed this a year ago in my blog. But failure was inevitable, especially set against the divisive messages and actions from the Government.

So, I prepare the somewhat complex operation of making the journey to Parliament. I hope thousands of us make it; we have so much stacked against us. The fact that we get to demonstrate on the street at all is something approaching miraculous.

I've been in the central lobby before, for the Hardest Hit march in 2011. They took away my whistle at security but I kept my banner. My MP, Emily Thornberry, came down to meet a bunch of us from Disability Action in Islington. It felt like she had a rehearsed speech; I was not impressed. I wonder how she will do today.

I lobby because there must be change. As part of our week, Reclaiming Our Futures, DPAC is delivering our manifesto, which is a reassertion for rights, for inclusion. I'm angry. Disabled people are not merely easy labels of vulnerability and need. We are human beings. Do I really have to keep spelling this out?

4 September 2013

⇨ The above information is reprinted with kind permission from *The Guardian*. Please visit www.guardian.co.uk for further information.

How aid is changing disabled people's lives in Uganda

After seeing the difference aid makes to the lives of disabled people in Uganda, Channel 4's Ade Adepitan is lobbying for disability rights to be included in the UN's millennium development goals.

Back in August I met with the minister for international development, Lynne Featherstone, writes Ade Adepitan. She told me about the UN's millennium development goals and how they were changing the world. They targeted many of the world's major issues, and the top line was 'Leave nobody behind'.

Surprisingly, the goals didn't include anything on disability. The MDGs are due for reassessment in 2015, and Lynne's aim is to lobby the UN to add disability rights to the goals when they're re-launched. She asked me to help her with the task.

Even though I was apprehensive, I felt this was a really important thing to do. It's estimated that around 70 million children in Africa are living with disabilities. 90 per cent of them do not regularly attend schools and they are also more likely to experience violence. It's easy to see why my parents left their friends and family in Nigeria and believed they had to bring me to the UK so I could have a better life.

Long distances

Two months after our meeting I flew to Uganda with Lynne and her team. Uganda has become one of the leading lights in Africa when it comes to disability rights issues. We went over to see how British aid and other projects were supporting disabled people.

After two eight-hour flights, we landed at Entebbe airport, an hour south of the capital Kampala. Once our paperwork was sorted, we flew for another hour towards the east of Uganda, to a town called Soroti. From Soroti we drove 35 km to Wera primary school. It has 901 pupils, 24 of them with disabilities.

Despite the school's size, there were only 14 teachers, who struggled to cope with the huge class sizes. We talked to the teachers and children about the challenges faced by the disabled pupils.

A common problem was travelling long distances to school: kids with weak lower limbs arrived to school physically exhausted. Add to this the school not being able to give them lunch and you begin to realise why 90 per cent of disabled children in Africa do not get regular schooling.

One parent carried his daughter Dorothy, who was blind and unable to walk, 2 km to school every day. He said he did it because he wanted to give his children a better life when they were older.

Mental strength

During our tour we were shown the school's only accessible toilet, built by UK-based charity Water Aid. It was basic but functional and, importantly, it had a ramp, and a door for privacy. Before this, disabled kids in the school had to crawl on the floor in the main toilets while being ridiculed by some of the able-bodied kids.

School in the UK can be hard, but I can't imagine what it's like to feel so degraded every time you need to go to the bathroom. I admired the mental strength of these children and their parents. They were prepared to go through this humiliation to get an education. Fortunately, thanks to the new toilet, at least part of their nightmare was over.

The next day we left the hotel at 7.45am and headed to the Kaberamaido district, a 45-minute drive from Soroti. The aim was to get there early so we could meet some of the beneficiaries of a Ugandan Government pilot scheme supported by DfID. The scheme provides a small amount of cash to vulnerable households, families with elderly members, and people with disabilities.

Life-changing differences

As it was explained to me, I could already hear the UK sceptics saying that this would create a culture of dependency, it would create scroungers. I wish they could have met some of the elderly Ugandans who, if eligible, received the equivalent of £5.

They used it to employ people to help with growing crops for food. There was a teenager who had had his leg amputated after an accident. He used the money to buy a prosthetic leg. There was a disabled lady who used the money to set up her clothes-making business. This money was being used to make life-changing differences in the lives of the most vulnerable in Uganda.

I spent three incredibly thought-provoking days in Uganda, and I'm very grateful to Lynne Featherstone for inviting me on the trip. It's made me realise how much important work needs to be done when it comes to disability rights.

I've been able to turn my dreams into reality. I can't imagine living in a place where you have no chance of succeeding because you're disabled. Unfortunately, this is the reality for millions of people. I hope that by including disability rights in the new set of UN millennium goals, we can begin to create a level playing field for people with disabilities all over the world.

31 October 2013

⇨ The above information is reprinted with kind permission from Channel 4 News. Please visit www.channel4.com/news for further information.

Key facts

- More than ten million people in the UK are disabled, 770,000 of whom are children. (page 1)

- 58% of people over 50 will have a long-term health condition by 2020. (page 1)

- Only 17% of disabled people are born with their disability. (page 1)

- Less than one in five people with a learning disability work (compared with one in two disabled people generally). (page 3)

- Just one in three people with a learning disability take part in some form of education or training. (page 3)

- 29,000 adults with a learning disability live with parents aged 70 or over, many of whom are too old or frail to continue in their caring role. (page 3)

- Seven out of ten families caring for someone with profound and multiple learning disabilities have reached or come close to 'breaking point' because of a lack of short-break services. (page 3)

- Dyslexia is a specific learning difficulty that affects approximately 10% of the UK population. (page 4)

- In England, it is estimated that one in every 100 children has an Autism Spectrum Disorder (ASD). (page 6)

- In 2011, the World Health Organization published the first *World Report on Disability*. They estimated that more than one billion people across the world, approximately 15% of the population, live with a disability. (page 10)

- In the UK, one in ten people live with a disability. (page 10)

- Adults with mental health issues are four times more likely to be victims of violent crime, and ten times more likely to be victims of hate crime than their non-disabled peers. (page 11)

- Disabled children are 57% more likely to be bullied and children with learning difficulties are four times more likely to be bullied or abused. (page 11)

- 72% of disabled people think that the Paralympics have had a positive impact on attitudes. 20% say it's changed the way people talk to them and 20% say it's made people more aware of their needs. (page 15)

- 54% of disabled people say they experience discrimination on a regular basis, with 84% of disabled people saying people patronise them and 63.5% saying thy have experienced people refusing to make adjustments or do things differently. (page 15)

- Nearly 10,000 children aged five to seven are acting as unpaid carers for family members or guardians, according to figures that have been published which were described by one children's charity as the tip of the iceberg. (page 20)

- The latest Census figures revealed that a total of 177,918 minors are carers for their loved ones, with 15,728 providing more than 50 hours of care a week and 19,422 between 20 and 49 hours. (page 20)

- 40% of carers care for their parents/parents-in-law. (page 21)

- Almost 40% of disabled people receiving social care support are not having their basic needs met, including eating, washing, dressing or getting out of the house. (page 23)

- 105,000 disabled people are at risk of not getting the basic support they need to help them eat, get washed and leave their homes. (page 24)

- 42% of disabled jobseekers cite employers' attitudes as a barrier to work. (page 32)

- 37% of disabled jobseekers cite transport difficulties as a barrier to work. (page 32)

- A study from the National Autistic Society, alongside Mencap, Scope, Sense and Leonard Cheshire Disability says that for every £1 spent on services, benefits to people, carers, local and central Government worth £1.30 are generated. (page 36)

Disability

The Equality Act 2010 defines a disabled person as anyone who has a physical or mental impairement that has a substantial and long-term adverse affect on his or her ability to carry out day-to-day activities. (NHS Choices, 2012). The nature of the disability will determine the extent to which it impacts on an individual's daily life. The definition of disability includes both physical impairments, such as multiple sclerosis or blindness, and learning disabilities such as autism.

Disability discrimination

The act of showing someone less favourable treatment (discriminating against them) because they have a disability. This may be through outright abusive behaviour, or by denying them access to employment, education or goods and services. The Equality Act 2010 states that it is illegal to discriminate against anybody because of a disability.

Disability Living Allowance (DLA)

DLA is tax-free benefit provided by the Government to help people with disabilities meet the costs of day-to-day life. Some disabilities mean that it is difficult or impossible to stay in regular employment, and it may also be necessary to meet the high cost of specialist equipment and care. Disability Living Allowance is provided to help cover these costs.

Hidden disabilities

Not all disabilities are obvious. An individual who suffers from epilepsy, mental ill health or diabetes still faces the challenge of coping with a disability but is often not recognised as a disabled person, since to a casual observer they do not display the outward symptoms often associated with disability.

Independent Living Fund

The Independent Living Fund (ILF) provided money to help disabled people live an independent life in the community, rather than having to rely on residential care. Payments from the ILF could be used to: employ a carer or personal assistant to give you personal and domestic care, or to pay a care agency to provide personal care and help with domestic duties. A group of five disabled people are currently arguing against the Government's decision to abolish the ILF, claiming that 20,000 severely disabled people have been left in extreme difficulty and that their views were not taken into account when the decision was made to halt payments from March 2015 and stop accepting new claims.

Learning disabilities

Learning disabilities, sometimes called learning disorders or difficulties (although these terms can have a wider definition and it would be incorrect to use them interchangeably with 'learning disability'), are defined by the World Health Organization as 'a state of arrested or incomplete development of mind'. Learning disabilities affect a person's ability to learn, communicate and carry out everyday tasks. Autism and Asperger Syndrome are two examples of learning disabilities. People with Down's Syndrome will also have a learning disability. Learning disabilities were referred to as 'mental handicaps' in the past, but this definition is now considered obsolete and offensive.

Paralympic Games

The Paralympic Games are a series of sporting competitions open to athletes with physical disabilities. They are held immediately following the Olympic Games. Athletes with disabilities including amputations, paralysis and blindness take part in a wide range of competitive sports. The most recent Paralympics was held in London in 2012.

Assignments

Brainstorming

⇨ In small groups, brainstorm what you know about disabilities. You should consider the following:

- What is a disability?
- What are some of the challenges that disabled people face?
- What is a learning disability?
- What is an ASD?

Research

⇨ Read the article on page two *What is a learning disability?* Choose one of the learning disabilities that are mentioned in the article and research it further, using the Internet or your local library. Write some notes that detail your findings and report back to your class with a short three-minute verbal presentation.

⇨ Research some of the apps that have been developed to help children with learning difficulties and create a five-minute PowerPoint presentation to show your class. You could, for example, look at apps used with children who have an autism spectrum disorder (ASD).

⇨ Individually, or with a partner, visit your local town and make a list of all the difficulties you might encounter if you were a wheelchair user. You should consider the accessibility of shops and public transport.

⇨ Research the challenges faced by disabled people in another country. The country you choose should be significantly different from the UK, e.g. Uganda, India, China, etc. Write a report based on your findings.

Design

⇨ Design a leaflet that could be distributed to parents, describing the indicators of dyslexia and dyscalculia and giving them information about what they can do if they think that their child has one of these learning difficulties.

⇨ Design an advertising campaign (TV or web-based) that will encourage young people with physical disabilities to get involved in sport. You might wish to research sporting facilities that are available in your area for those with physical disabilities.

Oral

⇨ Have the Paralympic Games improved daily life for disabled people? Discuss with a partner.

⇨ Do you think there is a stigma surrounding disability in the UK? Discuss in small groups.

⇨ Choose one of the illustrations from this book and, with a partner, discuss whether you feel it successfully represents the article it accompanies.

⇨ As a class, stage a debate in which half of you argue that the Government should put the Independent Living Fund back in place, and the other half argue that the Government was right to stop the scheme.

⇨ What could the Government do to improve employment opportunities for disabled people in the UK? Discuss with a partner.

Reading/writing

⇨ Read the article *Time to tackle labels in society* on page nine and write a blog post from the point of view of someone who believes that the term 'disability' should be banned. You should concentrate on making your post sound impassioned and persuasive.

⇨ The charity Mencap, for people with learning disabilities, was known in the past as The National Society for Mentally Handicapped Children, and before that as The National Association of Parents of Backward Children. Why do you think that labels we would now consider highly offensive towards people with disabilities were in the past considered not only acceptable but mainstream?

⇨ Write an article for your local newspaper, exploring the issues raised by the article *Thousands of children as young as five act as family carers, figures show* on page 20.

⇨ Write a summary of the employment and education rights of disabled people in the UK.

⇨ Read the article *What happens to older disabled people* on page 32. The article is from an American-based website, are there any aspects that are not relevant to the UK? Research further and write a similar article from the perspective of an elderly person in the UK.

⇨ Construct a PowerPoint presentation that explains the Equality Act 2010 and how it relates to people with disabilities.

⇨ Examine the treatment of disabled people throughout history. Use your research to create a timeline showing how attitudes to people with disabilities have changed.

Acknowledgements

The publisher is grateful for permission to reproduce the material in this book. While every care has been taken to trace and acknowledge copyright, the publisher tenders its apology for any accidental infringement or where copyright has proved untraceable. The publisher would be pleased to come to a suitable arrangement in any such case with the rightful owner.

Images

Cover, page iii and page 10: iStock, page 2: MorgueFile, Page 5 © Nial Bradshaw, page 13: iStock, pages 18 & 19 © George Hawkins, page 20: iStock, page 30: iStock, page 32: iStock, page 3: iStock, page 36: iStock, page 38: iStock.

Illustrations

Page 1: Don Hatcher, page 4: Angelo Madrid, page 14: Don Hatcher, page 17: Angelo Madird, pages 27 and 28: Simon Kneebone.

Additional acknowledgements

Editorial on behalf of Independence Educational Publishers by Cara Acred.

With thanks to the Independence team: Mary Chapman, Sandra Dennis, Christina Hughes, Jackie Staines and Jan Sunderland.

Cara Acred

Cambridge, January 2014